GOSPEL F✞UNDATIONS

God with Us

VOL. 5	THE GOSPELS

LifeWay Press® • Nashville, Tennessee

From the creators of *The Gospel Project*, Gospel Foundations is a six-volume resource that teaches the storyline of Scripture. It is comprehensive in scope yet concise enough to be completed in just one year. Each seven-session volume includes videos to help your group understand the way each text fits into the storyline of the Bible.

ISBN 978-1-5359-0362-2 • Item 005803636

Dewey decimal classification: 230
Subject headings: CHRISTIANITY / GOSPEL / SALVATION

Editorial Team

Michael Kelley
Director, Groups Ministry

Brian Dembowczyk
Managing Editor

Joel Polk
Editorial Team Leader

Daniel Davis, Josh Hayes
Content Editors

Brian Daniel
Manager, Short-Term Discipleship

Darin Clark
Art Director

We believe that the Bible has God for its author; salvation for its end; and truth, without any mixture of error, for its matter and that all Scripture is totally true and trustworthy. To review LifeWay's doctrinal guideline, please visit lifeway.com/doctrinalguideline.

To order additional copies of this resource, write to LifeWay Resources Customer Service; One LifeWay Plaza; Nashville, TN 37234; fax 615-251-5933; call toll free 800-458-2772; order online at LifeWay.com; email orderentry@lifeway.com; or visit the LifeWay Christian Store serving you.

Printed in the United States of America

Groups Ministry Publishing
LifeWay Resources
One LifeWay Plaza
Nashville, TN 37234

Contents

About *The Gospel Project*

Gospel Foundations is from the creators of *The Gospel Project*, which exists to point kids, students, and adults to the gospel of Jesus Christ through weekly group Bible studies and additional resources that show how God's plan of redemption unfolds throughout Scripture and still today, compelling them to join the mission of God.

The Gospel Project provides theological yet practical, age-appropriate Bible studies that immerse your entire church in the story of the gospel, helping to develop a gospel culture that leads to gospel mission.

Gospel Story

Immersing people of all ages in the storyline of Scripture: God's plan to rescue and redeem His creation through His Son, Jesus Christ.

Gospel Culture

Inspiring communities where the gospel saturates our experience and doubters become believers who become declarers of the gospel.

Gospel Mission

Empowering believers to live on mission, declaring the good news of the gospel in word and deed.

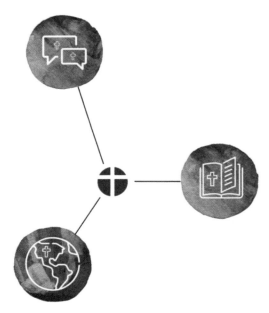

How to Use This Study

This Bible-study book includes seven weeks of content for group and personal study.

Group Study

Regardless of what day of the week your group meets, each week of content begins with the group session. Each group session uses the following format to facilitate simple yet meaningful interaction among group members and with God's Word.

Introducing the Study & Setting the Context
These pages include **content and questions** to get the conversation started and **infographics** to help group members see the flow of the biblical storyline.

Continuing the Discussion
Each session has a corresponding **teaching video** to help tell the Bible story. These videos have been created specifically to challenge the group to consider the entire story of the Bible. After watching the video, continue the **group discussion** by reading the Scripture passages and discussing the questions on these pages. Finally, conclude each group session with **a personal missional response** based on what God has said through His Word.

Personal Study

Three personal studies are provided for each session to take individuals deeper into Scripture and to supplement the content introduced in the group study. With **biblical teaching and introspective questions**, these sections challenge individuals to grow in their understanding of God's Word and to respond in faith.

Leader Guide

A tear-out leader guide for each session is provided on pages 95-108, which includes possible answers to questions highlighted with an icon and suggestions for various sections of the group study.

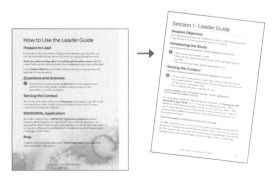

God's Word to You

A Son Was Born for You

Isaiah 9:6: "For a child will be born for us, a son will be given to us."

A Son will be given—a gift, a present. Isaiah lived in days shadowed by gloom, but God granted a flicker of hope, a ray of light—a Son would be given, a descendant of King David would come, an eternal kingdom would be established, one marked by justice and righteousness.

Yet God's people were shrouded in gloom for their lack of justice and righteousness. Their idolatry, their sin, brought God's judgment and their exile to the nations. They were meant to be a light to the nations; instead, they were nearly snuffed out. Still, a flicker of hope, a ray of light—a Child would be born. Through many dark days and years of God's silence, the flicker remained until the Son at last was given.

Matthew 1:21: "She will give birth to a son, and you are to name him Jesus, because he will save his people from their sins."

God presents His gift, the Son. And this Son answers the question, He solves the problem of their gloom—He will save His people from their sins. Their lack of justice and righteousness will be made up in His fullness. Their idolatry and sin will be done away with in His sacrifice. The flicker rages; the ray bursts forth; the Light has come to His people—and more.

Luke 2:10-11: "But the angel said to them, 'Don't be afraid, for look, I proclaim to you good news of great joy that will be for all the people: Today in the city of David a Savior was born for you, who is the Messiah, the Lord.'"

The present, the gift, is for all the people. The Savior from sins is for all the people; the Messiah-King is for all the people. Repent of your sin and believe in Jesus, who died for sins and rose from the dead that you may have life. "See, now is the acceptable time; now is the day of salvation!" (2 Cor. 6:2).

The Birth of Jesus

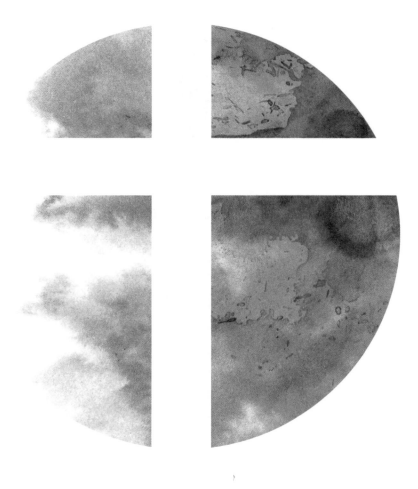

Introducing the Study

God left no doubt about what He expected from His people. As a jealous and loving God, He demanded holistic devotion that stemmed from the heart, not the halfhearted attempts of worship that were happening in the days of Malachi. The message of the Book of Malachi reminds us of our inability to love God because of our sin-tainted hearts, but we also hear the echoing promise of God to provide the coming Messiah, who would bring victory—true and lasting freedom—to His people.

 What do you think the four hundred years of silence between the Old and New Testaments was like for God's people?

The final words of the Old Testament are a curse, one that still hangs over sinful humanity. This curse cannot be lifted by our efforts. The only solution is a new heart rid of sin, and after four hundred years of silence, God provided the remedy for sin we need through the birth of a child, His Son, Jesus. The God whom humanity had sinned against would provide forgiveness of sin by taking on humanity Himself.

How does the storyline of Scripture change the way you view the birth of Jesus?

Setting the Context

The four hundred years between the end of the Old Testament and the beginning of the New Testament is referred to as **the intertestamental period** and included a lot of political turmoil for the Jews, but the one true God was still present and unchanging.

> What is the difference between God's silence and God's inactivity? Why is it important to recognize that difference?

The Persian Empire was conquered by **Alexander the Great** of Macedonia, who introduced Greek culture and the Greek language into the conquered territories of his empire. After Alexander's death, a series of successors ruled Judea. The most notorious, **Antiochus IV Epiphanes**, tried to destroy the Jewish religion. He forbade observance of the law and sacrificed a pig on the altar in the temple. This act of desecration fueled rebellion in Judea for years, and the result was **an independent Jewish state** for a time.

Then around 63 BC, **the Roman Empire** seized control. Two important religious and political groups emerged during this time. The Pharisees were committed to God's law, as supplemented by their own oral traditions. The Sadducees rejected most of the Old Testament and aligned themselves closely with Rome.

This was the climate in Judea when Jesus was born. In the fullness of time, in the fullness of Scripture, as **"Hearing the Old Testament in Jesus' Birth"** (p. 11) shows, God's Rescuer had come, though not to free His people from Rome but from sin.

> ✱ Why is it important to see the birth of Jesus in its context in the storyline of the Bible?

CHRIST Connection

The birth of Jesus fulfilled several Old Testament promises concerning the coming Messiah. Jesus was born in humble circumstances to be the Suffering Servant who would lay down His life to be our mighty Savior. One day, Jesus will return as our eternal King.

Hearing the **Old Testament** *in* **Jesus' Birth**

OLD TESTAMENT	NEW TESTAMENT
God Promised A Seed to Abraham (Gen. 12; 15; 17)	**Jesus** The Son of Abraham, the Seed (Matt. 1:1; Gal. 3:16)
God Promised A Descendant on David's Throne Forever (2 Sam. 7)	**Jesus** The Son of David, the Son of God (Matt. 1:1; Luke 1:32)
Immanuel A Sign Conceived by a Virgin (Isa. 7:14)	**God Is with Us** The Son Born to Mary, a Virgin (Matt. 1:18-23)
From Bethlehem Would Come God's Ruler over Israel (Mic. 5:2)	**In Bethlehem** The Messiah Was Born (Matt. 2:1-6; Luke 2:1-6)
A Star From Jacob, a Scepter from Israel (Num. 24:17)	**The King of the Jews** Heralded by a Star (Matt. 2:1-2,9-10)

Continuing the Discussion

Watch this session's video, and then continue the group discussion using the following guide.

The Book of Malachi left us wondering if the people of God would be ready for the Messiah. Were they? Why or why not?

How should a deeper understanding of the birth of Jesus affect the way we approach and prepare for a Christmas celebration?

As a group, read Luke 1:26-33.

Why is it important to see Jesus as the fulfillment of God's promises in the Old Testament?

What qualities of God's character are displayed in His choice of Mary?

God sent Gabriel to prepare Mary to be the mother of the Messiah. Mary was filled with both fear and awe in Gabriel's presence. The angel's message was troubling because of its supernatural nature, but at the same time it was filled with hope. Mary's Son would be great, He would be called "the Son of the Most High," and God would give Him the throne of David. The Baby whom Mary would deliver would be the fulfillment of God's centuries-old promise of a king from David's family who would establish an eternal kingdom.

As a group, read Luke 1:51-55.

How was Jesus' birth related to God's promise to Abraham?

What aspects of God's character and work did Mary highlight in her praise?

What examples of these aspects of God have you seen in your life?

Mary sang of future events with certainty as though they already had occurred, following the example of the Old Testament prophets. Mary described God's remarkable activity in bringing the Messiah to fulfill God's kingdom. Through His Messiah, God would humble the powerful and exalt the dispossessed. Mary was a prime example of God's lifting up a person of humble circumstances. She was symbolic of what God would do for all who would respond positively to His gift of grace.

As a group, read Luke 2:4-7.

> Why are the circumstances of Jesus' birth so surprising?

 What does the setting of Jesus' birth tell us about God's intent in sending Him?

Luke's record of Jesus' birth is simple yet magnificent. Luke frames Jesus' birth in historical terms while marveling in God's divine act of invading human history. God worked through the plans of government officials to bring Mary and Joseph to Bethlehem for Jesus' birth in fulfillment of Old Testament prophecy. He then used ordinary people to spread the extraordinary message of Christ's birth.

✝ MISSIONAL Application

Record in this space at least one way you will apply the truth of Scripture as one who believes in and follows after our humble Savior and King.

Personal Study 1

Jesus was born to be the promised eternal King.

Read Luke 1:26-33.

Luke addressed his Gospel to Theophilus. Though we are not certain who Theophilus was and why Luke wrote to him, we do know something about the author. Luke was a faithful companion of the apostle Paul. At the end of Paul's life, as he was facing the prospect of death under the Roman emperor Nero, only Luke had the courage to remain beside him (2 Tim. 4:11). This reveals much about the character of the writer of this Gospel.

We also know that Luke was a doctor, because Paul referred to him as one in Colossians 4:14. Luke was most likely a slave as well. Most professionals including doctors in the first century were slaves. It's not surprising then that Luke was interested in the most marginalized people of his day. Throughout his Gospel, Luke noted that women were often the first ones to understand what Jesus was doing. At the beginning of the Gospel, Zechariah, a religious man, didn't understand what God was going to do (though he should have). But Mary, a simple girl, intuitively understood what God was going to do (though we wouldn't expect her to).

Mary, who is twice described as a virgin, will give birth to Jesus. (The promise to Joseph is described in Matt. 1:18-25.) This poor, young, pregnant girl was the epitome of the marginalized.

Mary's promised child would be named Jesus. Traditionally, a father named his child, and in this case, God as the heavenly Father claimed that right over Joseph. The name Jesus means "deliverer" or "savior." Its Old Testament equivalent Hebrew name was Joshua. Just as Joshua, Moses' successor, delivered God's people by bringing them out of the wilderness and into the promised land, so would this new Joshua deliver God's people. Though this time, deliverance would not be from a place, but instead from sin and death and into eternal life with God.

Then the angel further clarified who Mary's son would be. Jesus would be the "Son of the Most High," affirming His divine identity. As a descendant of King David, Jesus would occupy the great king's throne to carry on the just and righteous reign of God on earth (see Isa. 9:7; Dan. 7:14). God was at long last making good on His promises.

He would be the One to crush the head of the serpent God promised Adam and Eve. He would be the blessing to all nations that God promised Abraham. He would be the bearer of the new covenant God promised through Jeremiah. And He would be the Messiah-King who would occupy the throne that God promised David.

All these promises and more are fulfilled in Jesus. Jesus is not only the promised eternal King; Jesus is the evidence that God keeps every one of His promises, both now and forever.

Why is it important that we recognize that Jesus is not only the king, but the promised king?

What are some of the practical implications for your life today in calling Jesus "King"?

Personal Study 2

Jesus was born to be the promised mighty Savior.

Read Luke 1:51-55.

How would Mary respond to the angel's dramatic pronouncement? With faith. Mary declared herself to be the slave of the Lord, her Master. This was her identity. After all, slaves have no choices; they are fully surrendered to their masters. Even though there was so much she did not know, Mary had a deep-rooted faith and trust in God. That was where her submissive spirit came from. She was ready to submit to God even if His plan for her life would be difficult.

Then Mary praised the greatness of God in the song that has become known as the "Magnificat." Mary's song concluded with a refrain that celebrates the truth that the world is being turned upside down—or more accurately, right side up. Radical reversal is Luke's favorite theme, and Mary presents it here in poetic form.

Mary's language reveals a heart and mind that must have been saturated with the psalms and songs of the Old Testament. For the moment, she has become a psalmist herself. And like David, she understood that the new hope being born into the world was based on an ancient hope.

Some of the psalms are referred to as "psalms of remembrance." When a psalmist lamented his current despair, he frequently looked back to the gracious acts of mercy God had performed in the past. Miriam, the sister of Moses (Mary's namesake), remembered in this way and, with a timbral in her hand, sang a song of new hope recorded in Exodus 15. Miriam celebrated the Lord God defeating Israel's enemies, that the horse and rider had been thrown into the sea. Mary's song in Luke might even be a refrain from Miriam's ancient poem.

The God of the Gospels is a God who is always in the process of turning the world upside down. The new hope that was being born, the hope that is the subject of so many songs in the Scriptures, was granted to everyone—even the outsiders, the poor in spirit. To be rich, we learn to let go of earthly treasures. To be wise, we embrace the foolishness of the cross. To be mature, we become like little children. To be free, we become slaves to God. All of this happens through Jesus who, though born in lowly circumstances, was the exalted mighty Savior.

Jesus won everything by losing everything. Paul said He was crucified in weakness (2 Cor. 13:4). Yet in the mysterious ways of God, the cross has granted endless strength to those who have suffered and are suffering still.

This is the radical reversal, the "upside-down-ness" of the kingdom that the church easily forgets. Every time she has pursued worldly power, forsaking worldly weakness, the church has parted company with Jesus. God is not magnified in that way. He is magnified by the pierced soul of His people, emulating the pierced hands and feet of their Savior. God is glorified when the church treasures Christ above all else and lives with meekness, even if that leads to suffering. Because suffering—that which Christ endured on the cross—is what brought about the ultimate reversal of sin and death giving way to forgiveness and eternal life for those who trust in the One Mary sang of.

Compare Mary's song with Miriam's song in Exodus 15 and Hannah's song in 1 Samuel 2. How does Mary's song build on these older songs?

How does your life challenge the values of the world with the values of the kingdom?

Personal Study 3

Jesus was born to be the promised humble Servant.

Read Luke 2:4-7.

The birth of the promised King and the mighty Savior was inauspicious to say the least. But Luke does not sidestep the surprising circumstances of Jesus' birth in his Gospel; he focuses on them. The humble birth of Jesus advances the major theme of radical reversal.

Throughout his portrayal of the life and ministry of Jesus, Luke reveals that those who should have understood Jesus' ministry rarely did. The wealthy, the educated, and the most religious missed what was happening. At the same time, those whom you'd never expect to understand what God was doing—the women, the poor, the marginalized—intuitively grasp what Jesus' coming meant.

Jesus was born during the reign of Augustus. Julius Caesar had adopted Augustus as a son, making him his heir. But there is more to the story than a simple transfer of power. Upon his death, Caesar was declared to be divine. A comet appeared shortly afterward that supposedly affirmed his deity.

Luke's first readers would have been reminded that the emperor was considered to be the son of the divine, that is, "a son of God." But meanwhile, in the obscure Judean town of Bethlehem, a baby was about to be born who would literally challenge the most powerful empire in the world and inaugurate a kingdom that would eclipse Rome's.

Jesus was born into a world that was turning upside down. A clue to this shift is seen in the order of a census. In the process of taking power and transforming the empire, Augustus wanted to know the numbers, the value of property, and the distribution of the population. Quirinius was willing to oblige.

Luke recounts the nativity of Jesus in four simple verses. Joseph made the trip from Galilee south to Bethlehem, a town in the shadow of one of Herod's fortresses. Mary, his pregnant fiancée, was there with him. The two made the journey in obedience to the order to be counted in their hometown.

While there, Jesus is born and Mary wrapped Him in strips of cloth, or rags. Mary then placed her child in a feeding trough that would have been located in a cave or basement of a house in Bethlehem. Because the guest room was already filled, the family had to move into the stable. But even in this, we see the provision of God. It is warm and dry there. For the time being, the three of them will be safe. (Matthew tells us they later would flee for their lives.)

So, here we are struck with God not just becoming human, but that He was also born in a stable. The One through whom God made all that was made was born for us in poverty, without a proper place to lay His head. This "outsider" aura would follow Jesus the rest of His life. Jesus would fulfill His role as the humble Servant. He was born as a humble Servant, he would live as a humble Servant, and He would die as a humble Servant—all in full obedience to His Father.

But that humble Servant reigns as King of kings and Lord of lords. In Jesus, we see that the last shall be first, and the least shall be the greatest.

What do we learn from the way Luke contrasted the power and authority of Caesar Augustus with the birth of Jesus?

What do the humble circumstances of Jesus' birth teach us about God's authority and power?

The Preparation of Jesus

Introducing the Study

God's long promised rescue from sin and death was coming. But the rescue—and the Rescuer—had not burst onto the scene with great fanfare. Instead, Jesus was born in the most humble way imaginable: to a common family and in a stable. But this inauspicious birth was nevertheless the fulfillment of God's promises reaching back to the garden of Eden.

> How do the circumstances of Jesus' birth reflect His identity and mission in the world?

Looking back to the Old Testament, we see that the coming of Jesus was in no way haphazard or rushed. Instead, God had been preparing the world for the advent of His Son from the very beginning. Once born, God continued to prepare the way for His ministry and His message. Though Jesus was born in obscurity, He would soon step onto the public scene and change the world forever.

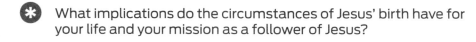 What implications do the circumstances of Jesus' birth have for your life and your mission as a follower of Jesus?

Setting the Context

Mary and Joseph lived in Nazareth, but they were in Bethlehem when Jesus was born because of the Roman census. They stayed there for a time until an angel appeared to Joseph in a dream telling him to flee to Egypt to protect Jesus from King Herod, and they lived in Egypt until Herod died. Then they returned to Nazareth. These are the only details we know of **Jesus' young childhood**, but the Bible describes this time in simple but profound terms: "The boy grew up and became strong, filled with wisdom, and God's grace was on him" (Luke 2:40).

 Why do you think the Bible does not provide us with much information about the early years of Jesus' life?

The only other glimpse into Jesus' boyhood involved one of the family's yearly trips to Jerusalem for Passover. When **Jesus was twelve**, He stayed behind in the temple while His parents started the journey back to Nazareth. When they realized He was not with them, they returned to Jerusalem and found Him in the temple, sitting with the teachers, amazing them with His questions and understanding of Scripture. And His explanation for His actions: "It was necessary for me to be in my Father's house" (2:49), reflecting the truth that **"Jesus Is God"** (p. 23). The rest of Jesus' growing up is summarized like this: "Jesus increased in wisdom and stature, and in favor with God and with people" (2:52).

In what ways do you think God prepared Jesus for His earthly ministry as He grew up?

✝ CHRIST Connection

God declared that Adam was good, yet Adam failed to obey God, and the entire world experienced the consequences of his sin. Jesus is the Second Adam, and God declared Him pleasing because Jesus overcame temptation, refused to doubt, and lived a life of perfect obedience to the Father. Jesus' obedience and faithfulness to the Father is what led Him to the cross, the place where He conquered the sin brought on by Adam and showed He is the Savior of the world.

Jesus *Is* God

Preexistent	• In the beginning, the Word was with God, and the Word was God; all of creation was made through Him—the Word became flesh (John 1:1-3,14) • John the Baptist testified that the One who came after him—Jesus—existed before him (John 1:14-15)
The Son of God	• Conceived in Mary by the Holy Spirit, therefore called the Son of God (Matt. 1:18,20; Luke 1:35) • The fulfillment of the name "Immanuel," which means "God is with us" (Matt. 1:22-23) • The voice from heaven proclaimed about Jesus at His baptism: "You are my beloved Son" (Mark 1:11)
Worthy of Worship Quoting the Old Testament, Jesus Himself said worship should only be given to the Lord God (Matt. 4:10)	• The wise men worshiped Jesus at His home in Bethlehem and gave Him gifts (Matt. 2:9-11) • Jesus' disciples worshiped Him after He walked on the water and came to them in their boat (Matt. 14:33) • The women at Jesus' tomb worshiped Him after seeing His resurrection (Matt. 28:9)
Yahweh of the Old Testament	• John the Baptist was God's messenger to prepare His way in the person of Jesus (Mark 1:2,4; Mal. 3:1) • John the Baptist's mission was to "prepare the way for the Lord," who is Jesus (Mark 1:3-4; Isa. 40:3-5)

Continuing the Discussion

 Watch this session's video, and then continue the group discussion using the following guide.

How would you describe the character and role of John the Baptist in God's story? What do we learn from him?

What do we learn about battling temptation from Jesus' encounter with Satan in the wilderness?

As a group, read Mark 1:1-8.

How do you think John saw himself based on these verses? What can we learn from the way he viewed himself?

 How would you explain repentance to a non-Christian?

God used John the Baptist as a spokesman—a prophet who would announce the arrival of Jesus and call on the people to prepare to meet their King through repentance. To repent means to turn from sin and ourselves and to God. This is a message we continue to preach. Like the people of Judea in John the Baptist's day, we too must prepare ourselves to meet Jesus by turning from sin and to Him.

As a group, read Mark 1:9-11.

 Why was Jesus baptized even though He didn't need to repent of sin?

What is so significant about the voice of God from heaven as Jesus was baptized?

Why is baptism an important step for followers of Jesus today?

Jesus' baptism signaled the beginning of His public ministry. Jesus was not baptized for the forgiveness of sin—He committed no sin requiring such forgiveness—but to identify Himself and His ministry with the ministry and message of John the Baptist. When Jesus was baptized in the river that day, He also identified with sinners who repented and believed. Likewise, we associate ourselves with the people of God and share our commitment to Him when we are baptized. God was pleased with His Son for His obedience, and when we repent of sin and believe in Christ, God pronounces the same affirmation over us.

As a group, read Matthew 4:1-11.

> Why is it significant that the Spirit led Jesus into the wilderness to be tempted by the devil?

✱ How was the temptation of Jesus similar to and different from the temptation Adam and Eve experienced in the garden?

Because Jesus trusted God, He followed the Spirit's leading, even though it meant being led into battle. Three times Satan tempted Jesus to trust in Himself rather than the Father, and three times Jesus combated the temptation with His faith in God's true Word. Where Adam and Eve failed in temptation, Jesus triumphed.

✝ MISSIONAL Application

Record in this space at least one way you will apply the truth of Scripture as a repentant believer in Christ who will follow the leading of the Holy Spirit.

Personal Study 1

The Son's messenger prepares the way for Him.

Read Mark 1:1-8.

The king God promised through the prophets finally arrived, but those expecting His coming must have been surprised. What they got was not what they had expected. They had hoped for a political messiah—a king who would overthrow the chains of Roman oppression. A leader of the right pedigree who could unite the people of Israel against their common foe. But that was not who Jesus would be. And the first clue that He would be different was found in His messenger, John.

Every king needs a herald—a representative to go before him and alert people that they are about to be in the presence of royalty. But some representative John was. He was not part of Israel's religious system—he had removed himself from it. He didn't live in Jerusalem—the epicenter of Jewish life; he lived in the wilderness. He didn't wear priestly garments; he wore animal skins. He didn't eat a priestly diet; he ate insects.

And yet, this unlikely prophet appealed to the common people. Why? Precisely because he was different from the religious leaders of the day. John was humble; they were proud. John's location, attire, and diet indicated how little he was concerned for his own benefit. The Pharisees and Sadducees, however, were quite concerned about their places of power and prominence.

But what stood out most about this unlikely prophet was his message. John called for repentance. At first glance, this was nothing new. The Jews had long touted repentance as the proper response to the presence of God. They believed repentance was the way to prepare to meet the coming Messiah.

John's ministry was unique though because of why he called people to repentance and whom he called to repentance. Why repent? To prepare the way for the arrival of the King. John called people to repentance so they would have eyes to see His works and ears to hear His teaching. Much like kings would have teams go before them to make ready the paths for their entourage to pass through a region, God sent John as an engineer to prepare hearts and minds of His people to welcome the coming King.

Whom did John call to repentance? Everybody. And that was scandalous. Calling sinners and pagans to repent was expected, but John called on the religious—the Pharisees and Sadducees—to repent as well. All of Israel had to turn away from the broken system of religion of the day. They had to turn away from the primary source of their identity. They had to reject worship as they knew it and prepare to encounter the source of true worship. John knew that the religious leaders especially needed to prepare themselves—their hearts and spirits were not right.

This unlikely prophet pointed to an unlikely Messiah. His gospel, literally "good news," was that the prophesied Messiah was finally here. The Gospel of Matthew highlights Jesus as the promised "Immanuel," meaning "God is with us" (Matt. 1:23). Jesus is the one divine King, the promised Messiah, and John bore witness to Him.

John understood his place in the story, and His place was one of preparation for Jesus. Jesus held the place of true greatness. Jesus was the center of the story. And Jesus would bring about a repentance John could only point to.

The Messiah—the Rescuer, the Deliverer, the Promised One, and the King—had come. It was time for His people to respond accordingly.

What stands out to you regarding John the Baptist's heralding of the arriving King?

What does this teach us about God's kingdom that might be unexpected?

Personal Study 2

The Father declares His pleasure with the Son.

Read Mark 1:9-11.

John the Baptist came preparing the people for the arrival of Jesus. But Jesus would not be the conquering king the people expected; God had sent the Suffering Servant prophesied by Isaiah. The people of Israel needed to understand the humility of their king, but they needed to understand His greatness as well. John confessed that he was not even worthy to untie the sandals of the One coming.

Jesus' hometown was nothing to brag about, consistent with the circumstances of His birth. Nazareth was a backwater village, the wrong side of the tracks which nothing of notoriety ever came from. Jesus left this remote village of no reputation and was baptized by John to begin His earthly ministry.

But why? We know from John's message that he was calling everyone everywhere to repentance, and that the sign of repentance was baptism. But Jesus was—and is—the perfect Son of God. He had no need to repent of sin because He was not a sinner. So why be baptized by John?

Jesus' baptism was, first of all, an issue of obedience to the Father. In the Book of Matthew, we see that John did not want to baptize Jesus because of His greatness. Who was he, John—the forerunner, to baptize Jesus the Messiah? If anyone was baptizing anyone, it should be the other way around. But Jesus explained that His baptism was not for sin, but rather to obey the commands of the prophets. Even from the beginning of His ministry, we see Jesus' priority was to do exactly what God had sent Him to do.

But there was another reason for Jesus' baptism. He was baptized to identify with sinners. Though Jesus was not a sinner, He was to be counted among the sinners. By being baptized as sinners were baptized, Jesus associated with those who needed to repent and believe. A few years after this, He would identify in a deeper, more profound way, when He would take the sins of the world on Himself at the cross. He who knew no sin would become sin so that we might be given His righteousness (2 Cor. 5:21).

So Jesus, the perfect Son of God, went down into the water and came back up. It was a shadow of what was to come. Jesus would go down into death as the sacrifice for sin and come back up, raised to new life never again to die.

Jesus identified with sinners in obedience to the will and plan of His Father, and His Father expressed His pleasure. The text tells us that immediately the heavens were torn open and the Spirit descended on Jesus like a dove. And the Father pronounced His approval: "You are my beloved Son; with you I am well-pleased" (Mark 1:11).

This same pronouncement that was given to Jesus because of His perfect obedience is credited to us because of that same obedience. When we believe in Jesus, His perfect righteousness is credited to our account, and we are positioned as the children of God.

How amazing to hear this from on high. How amazing to be adopted into God's family, co-heirs with Christ. How amazing to be counted righteous in Christ. How amazing to know that God has not made a mistake when He formed us and when He called us into His family. How amazing to hear, because of the gospel, "This is My beloved Son in whom I am well pleased!"

Why is it important to remember that Jesus' priority was obedience to the Father?

What practical difference does it make to you, as a Christian, to know that your Father in heaven is pleased with you?

Personal Study 3

The Spirit leads the Son into the wilderness to be tempted.

Read Matthew 4:1-11.

At the baptism of Jesus, the Father affirmed the identity of Jesus as His beloved Son, and the Spirit descended upon Him like a dove. The Spirit then led Jesus into the wilderness to be tempted. And not surprisingly, the first temptation centered on Jesus' identity as the Son of God—the affirmation just pronounced at His baptism.

In connecting these two stories, the Gospel writers help us see the line between the Jordan River and the desert. The baptism is the door to the wilderness.

God uses the wilderness to establish His people's identity as His sons and daughters. In the Old Testament, God called His people to the wilderness so they could learn His worth and learn to truly worship Him. The same can be said of the wilderness temptation of Jesus. Jesus' obedience in the wilderness demonstrated what it means to be a child of God.

We experience the same. Sometimes we go from the mountaintop to the valley—from the good times to the wilderness—because only there, in the spiritual desert, do we learn the worth of God. Only there do we learn how to trust God when it is difficult. And there we demonstrate our identity as His sons and daughters.

The wilderness temptation represents an all-out assault on the identity of Jesus, which was revealed at His baptism. It was a threefold attack. First, Satan tempted Jesus to satisfy His desires apart from the will of God—to sustain His life with physical bread. Jesus triumphed when He spoke of relying on the word of God for life.

Second, Satan tempted Jesus to test God's promise of protection by jumping from the roof of the temple. Once more, Jesus displayed His total trust in the Father and refuted Satan's attack with Scripture.

Third, the Devil tempted Jesus to abandon the identity the Father bestowed upon Him at the Jordan, the radical identification with the world that would finally lead Him to the cross. Jesus' final triumph in the wilderness occurred when He determined to serve and worship the Father alone and triumphed over the temptation of Satan.

This is not simply an ancient story of a struggle between good and evil. It is a battle plan for those who long to remain obedient to God. Jesus' victory in the wilderness matters because it is a foretaste of the victory He would achieve for the world on the cross. He is always the pattern and the paradigm. We have failed to engage or understand this narrative if we have not realized that His victory can be echoed in our own experience. His victory is ours! In light of Christ's work, our appropriate response is following His pattern of obedience as worship.

When have you had a "wilderness" experience in your life spiritually? Did it feel like a test? Why or why not?

How does Jesus' victory over temptation give you confidence when you are in the wilderness?

The Miracles of Jesus

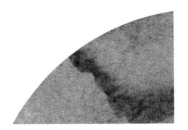

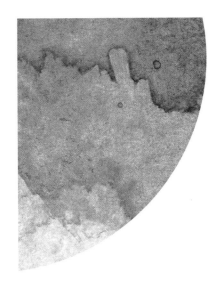

Introducing the Study

Jesus' public ministry began with an affirmation by His Father and an attack by Satan. The Son of God prevailed where all humanity had failed, but it would not be the last time Jesus squared off against the enemy. Jesus had maintained His trust in the Father and obeyed His will. This same trust and obedience would carry Jesus forward on His trajectory to the cross as the Savior of the world.

 How should the temptations of Jesus influence the way we view God's Word?

John had prepared Jesus' way, the Father had pronounced His approval, and now the Son had passed the test and would begin His public ministry. But as with His birth and baptism, Jesus' ministry would bring as much confusion and controversy as it did hope. As He began to travel, minister, and teach, Jesus embodied the mission and plan of God. He would, through His work and His miracles, show us the nature of God's kingdom and reveal His own identity to those willing to see.

What, in your mind, was the purpose of Jesus' miracles?

Setting the Context

John the Baptist, the forerunner of the Messiah, came upon hard days after the baptism of Jesus. He was arrested, imprisoned, and eventually beheaded by Herod.

Meanwhile, Jesus, having resisted the temptation of the enemy in the wilderness, began His **public ministry in Galilee**, the northernmost province in Palestine. Jesus would center most of His ministry there.

 In what ways might Jesus' wilderness experience have prepared Him to continue to walk in obedience to God's will?

Jesus also began the process of **calling His first disciples**, those who would follow Him closely for the next three years. Though they did not understand all the implications, men like Peter, Andrew, James, and John began to follow Jesus into the unknown.

As Jesus traveled, His basic message was the two-pronged message of the gospel—**repent and believe**. He also spoke extensively on **the kingdom of God** and performed **miracles** among the people. The Jewish people had longed for this, but there was a great deal of misunderstanding about the identity and purpose of Jesus in fulfilling the kingdom of God. **"Jesus' Signs in the Gospel of John"** (p. 35) reveals the purpose and result of some of Jesus' miracles, along with some of the positive and negative responses.

Which of the miracles of Jesus are most meaningful to you? Why?

✝ CHRIST Connection

From the very beginning of Jesus' earthly ministry, the people recognized that He was different, largely because of the power and authority He demonstrated through His miracles. Jesus' miracles proved He is the Son of God and also revealed His love and compassion for the people whom He came to save.

Jesus' Signs
in the Gospel of John

MIRACLE	PURPOSE	RESULT
FIRST SIGN: Turning Water into Wine (John 2:1-12)	Revealed Jesus' glory as the Son of God	Jesus' disciples believed in Him
SECOND SIGN: Healing an Official's Son (John 4:46-54)	—	The royal official and his household believed in Jesus
THIRD SIGN: Healing a Man Disabled for 38 Years (John 5:1-18)	Demonstrated Jesus' unity with the Father and authority over the Sabbath	The Jews began persecuting Jesus
FOURTH SIGN: Feeding of 5,000 (John 6:1-15)	Demonstrated Jesus, the bread of life, was greater than Moses (John 6:32-35)	The crowd wanted to make Jesus king by force, but He withdrew from them
FIFTH SIGN: Walking on Water (John 6:16-21)	Demonstrated Jesus' identity as "I AM"	—
SIXTH SIGN: Healing a Man Born Blind (John 9)	Displayed God's works in the man's healing	The man believed in Jesus and worshiped Him
SEVENTH SIGN: Raising Lazarus from the Dead (John 11)	Displayed God's glory and glorified the Son of God	Many believed in Jesus, but the Sanhedrin plotted to kill Him

Continuing the Discussion

▶ Watch this session's video, and then continue the group discussion using the following guide.

What were some of the ways people misunderstood the miracles of Jesus?

Why is it important to note that the miracles of Jesus were intended to reveal His identity and character?

As a group, read Mark 1:21-28.

What does it mean to say that Jesus taught with authority?

✳ Why were the miracles of Jesus essential to His authority?

Capernaum, on the northwestern shore of the Sea of Galilee, became Jesus' home base. From the beginning, people recognized that Jesus was different. Unlike other teachers who never gave an independent opinion but relied on another teacher's authority, Jesus taught with His own authority. His message was not validated by someone else but by the miracles He performed.

As a group, read Mark 1:35-38.

What does this practice of Jesus teach us about the nature and necessity of prayer?

How did the disciples' priorities differ from Jesus' in this scene?

✳ What can we learn about how Jesus viewed His mission from these verses?

After a hectic day of helping others, Jesus needed to be alone and pray. While Jesus was concerned about focusing on the mission God had given Him, the disciples seemed to be caught up in the increasing acclaim the people were giving Him. But Jesus was not concerned with being popular. His primary mission was to preach the good news. The miracles of healing and casting out of demons were secondary—a conduit to present the gospel and lead people to respond to that good news.

As a group, read Mark 1:39-42.

How did the leper in this passage express faith?

 Why is it significant that Jesus was moved to compassion and reached out and touched the man?

The man must have recognized that Jesus was a person of authority and power and that He could make him clean. Being made clean represented a number of things in this context. It stood for removal of a disease, spiritual purification, and normal living. The man trusted Jesus to make it happen, and Jesus did. In an act of compassion, Jesus reached out and touched the untouchable. Jesus' miracles were to reveal the gospel, but they also reflected His love for people.

✝ MISSIONAL Application

Record in this space at least one way you will apply the truth of Scripture as one who has experienced Jesus' power and compassion in salvation from sin.

Personal Study 1

Jesus' miracles proclaim His power and authority.

Read Mark 1:21-28.

The ministry of Jesus Christ was centered on the kingdom of God—God's reign in fulfillment of His promises to His people. Jesus did not just teach about the kingdom of God, He also displayed the nature and values of that kingdom through His miracles. Both of these elements of Jesus' ministry—His teaching and His miracles—worked hand-in-hand with each other. Jesus proclaimed the kingdom and demonstrated the kingdom, and in each one He revealed His place at the center of that kingdom.

In these verses, we see that Jesus' teaching took people by surprise. The crowds were amazed specifically at the authority of Jesus in His teaching. They realized that the way Jesus taught communicated something about Him. Jesus taught as one having authority, not as the teachers of the law.

Rabbis were highly educated. They knew centuries' worth of religious tradition inside and out. They had studied all the religious opinions, but they did not teach as if they had authority. They always appealed to the authority of religious tradition. The rabbis quoted the experts. Teaching from the rabbis was like listening to someone read an extended footnote. But Jesus was different. He didn't appeal to footnotes for authority. He positioned His teaching as authoritative on its own.

This was astonishing. Jesus was only thirty years old—not very old by the standards of the ancient world. He had grown up in Nazareth, a small town of little importance, not Jerusalem, the hub of religious life. He was a carpenter, not a Sadducee, Pharisee, or lawyer. He had not gone to the schools the rabbis attended. And yet Jesus spoke with an authority that exceeded that of the older scribes who had the right credentials.

Jesus even taught differently than the Old Testament prophets. The prophets had not spoken with their own authority either. But they didn't appeal to other prophets; they appealed to God as they introduced their messages by saying, "Thus says the LORD." They spoke with the authority of God. But Jesus never used that phrase. He spoke with His own authority when He interpreted or reapplied the law, when He made promises, when He commanded, and when He prohibited. The people had never heard anyone do that before. Jesus' teachings were powerful. Yet He was not a rabbi. He was not a prophet. What was He?

And this is where His miracles factored in. Jesus demonstrated the authority of His words by the power of His works. Anyone could say whatever he or she wanted. But could anyone do what Jesus did?

While Jesus was teaching, He was interrupted by the cries of a man possessed by unclean spirits. But these were not wordless exclamations; in fact, the question the man asked, born from the demonic, reveals that demons knew more about this new teacher than the people listening to Him. And these demons knew that the authority and mission of Jesus would bring judgment. He didn't need to appeal to a greater power or use some authoritative incantation to cast out the demons; He simply uttered a command. He was the ultimate authority, and He exercised that authority over the spirits. Once again, the people were amazed. They had never experienced anything like this—a teacher who not only taught with authority but who backed up His teaching with authoritative action.

This same Jesus who spoke and acted in power and authority is the One we worship today. Just as He had authority in word and deed then, He holds the same power over us and our circumstances today. But like the people in Capernaum, we must not only marvel at the power of Jesus; we must recognize His authority and submit our lives to it.

What are some ways we as Christians fall short of living under Jesus' authority and can merely be impressed with His teaching?

Is there anything causing you to question either the power or authority of Jesus? What is God calling you to do instead?

Personal Study 2

Jesus' miracles reveal His greater purpose.

Read Mark 1:35-38.

Jesus' authority, as displayed in both His teaching and His miraculous power, certainly generated great discussion among the people and His fame spread like a brush fire in a dry climate. Word of this upstart rabbi swept through the communities of Palestine. The whole town of Capernaum showed up for an audience with Jesus after they heard of His teaching and miracles. By the end of the day, Jesus had healed many people of their diseases and cast out demons. It had been a full day to say the least.

The next morning, Jesus went off alone to pray. The Son of God consistently made time to pray during His earthly ministry. Jesus would set aside everyone and everything to be with the Father (Mark 6:46; 14:32-41). Most of us should feel crushing conviction of how little we prioritize prayer in comparison.

But why did Jesus pray? He prayed because He knew that this was just the beginning. The crowds would grow. The pressure would mount. The temptation to veer from the will of God would increase. He needed these times of prayer to continue in His ministry and stay focused on the mission and will of the Father. But His disciples had other ideas.

Maybe they were excited by the crowds. Perhaps they sensed momentum on their side. Maybe they loved the popularity they experienced in town. Whatever the reason, the disciples interrupted Jesus' time of prayer and tried to draw Him back to those crowds. But Jesus had a greater purpose in mind.

Jesus would not return to the crowds from before; instead, He would press on to the neighboring villages. Rather than taking advantage of the popularity that lay before Him, He continued to pursue the mission God had given Him. He wasn't interested in being a popular miracle worker; He came to preach the good news of the kingdom.

For Jesus, His miracles were secondary; they served the greater purpose of His message. While Jesus was compassionate and wanted to alleviate the pain and suffering of others, He was more concerned to deal with the deeper disease that all humanity suffers from—sin and death. Jesus' message was one of the cure of sin through grace, and how through Him humanity might become right with God once again.

All His miracles ultimately point to this revelation. All His works of power and authority were meant to point to His ability and willingness to forgive sin.

Jesus' focus on His God-given mission reminds us to examine why we seek after Jesus. Are we, like the crowds at Capernaum, coming to Him because of what we think He can do for us? Are we looking to Him to change our current circumstances? Or have we recognized the true identity of the Son of God and come to Him in submission— in worship with gratitude for what He has already done for us?

What is the danger in seeking Jesus because of what we think He might be able to do for us?

How should we understand the place of Jesus' miracles given His focus on mission?

Personal Study 3

Jesus' miracles demonstrate His compassion.

Read Mark 1:39-42.

In biblical times, the word *leprosy* was used as a catch-all for many different skin diseases. But regardless of which skin disease a person suffered from, they all had the same effect. According to the law, a person with leprosy had to wear clothing that signified he had the disease and shout, "Unclean! Unclean!" as he approached others. Those with leprosy were forbidden to come in contact with anyone else because then that person would also be considered unclean. Leprosy took a physical toll on a person, but perhaps its emotional and social toll was worse. The disease made you a community pariah, shut off from everyone else.

Imagine waking up day after day and knowing that not a single person would look you in the eye, much less give shake your hand in friendship. Imagine knowing that you were the constant subject of sideways glances as mothers hurried their children out of your path. Imagine being known not for your talent, not for your personality, not for your kindness or anything else, but instead only being known for your disease. And imagine that you had to announce that identity over and over again: "Unclean! Unclean!"

This was the death this leper experienced every day of his life. But on this particular day, he did not follow the law. Instead of keeping his distance from Jesus, he came directly to Him, fell on his knees, and cried out for Jesus to do what only Jesus could do—to make him clean. This man didn't just want to be healed; he wanted to be clean. To be put back in right order. To be restored to the community that was around him but did not include him. And the leper knew Jesus could do it. The question, at least in his mind, was not whether or not Jesus was powerful enough to make him clean; it was whether or not he was willing. So how would Jesus respond to this unexpected interruption?

With Jesus' response we see an unthinkable act of One driven by compassion. This man was not an obstacle to His mission to preach the good news of the kingdom. The compassion He felt for this man was a hallmark of that very kingdom, rooted in God's self-determined compassion for sinful humanity that led to Jesus' arrival in the first place. Rather than ignoring the man, rather than turning away from him in disgust, rather than rebuking him for not following the law or interrupting Him, Jesus reached out to the man and touched him.

Notice that Jesus didn't heal the man's skin disease first and then touch Him. The Son of God bent low and placed His hands on the man's diseased body. Perhaps this was the first touch the leper had felt for months or even years. And in touching Him, Jesus violated the ceremonial law that had kept the man at a distance from other people. But in His touch, Jesus revealed that in the kingdom, love and compassion rule above ritual and regulation.

Praise the Lord it is so—not only for the leper, but for us as well. Jesus did not keep us, in our sinful uncleanness, at an arm's length. No, He bent low to us, so low that He came from heaven and was born as a servant, immersing Himself in sinful humanity (while Himself remaining sinless). We, like the leper, have experienced the authority, power, and love of Christ in His compassion. And because we have, there must be no one among us who is too unclean for us to go to as well. None are off limits. For through us, the Savior is still extending His compassionate hands.

Can you relate to the leper? When is a time that you have felt unclean and yet sensed the touch of Jesus?

Is there any group of people that you would deem too unclean for you to be around? What are the implications of Jesus' interaction for how you see those people?

The Teachings of Jesus

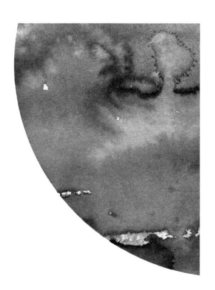
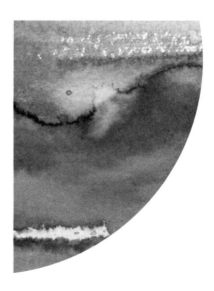

Introducing the Study

Jesus' fame began to grow. Crowds began to form as people anticipated encountering the One who taught with an authority no one had ever experienced and who performed such marvelous signs and wonders. But Jesus was never arbitrary in His words or His deeds. Everything He said and did served the greater purpose of revealing Himself as God's chosen Messiah, the Savior of the world.

What do Jesus' miracles reveal about His identity and character?

Jesus' ministry generated amazing popularity, but it created just as much controversy. One of the reasons was that Jesus associated with people who were considered to be outcasts and therefore off limits to religious people. Instead of shunning these people as the religious community expected, Jesus welcomed them and even positioned them as positive examples in His teaching. Jesus wanted everyone—from the greatest to the least—to understand that God was on a mission to seek and to save the lost and that He was overjoyed with any sinner who came home.

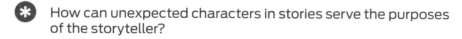 **How can unexpected characters in stories serve the purposes of the storyteller?**

Setting the Context

✳ What is the relationship between words and deeds?

Jesus taught with authority backed up by His miracles, but what was the substance of that teaching? While Jesus taught on a variety of subjects, several themes were repeated in His teaching as He traveled throughout Palestine.

One unique characteristic of His stories was His use of **unexpected heroes**. Instead of positioning religious Jewish men at the center of His stories, Jesus often held up Gentiles, women, or even children as having characteristics that should be emulated.

Furthermore, Jesus emphasized **the role of the heart** in His teaching. The religious system of the day was oppressive for the people, and to make matters worse, the religious leaders took advantage of loopholes and lived in open hypocrisy. But when Jesus taught, He cut through the external obligations and focused on the heart.

One more distinct component to Jesus' teaching was His use of **parables**, a common form of teaching in Judaism to communicate rich meaning through memorable symbolism. Jesus, however, said that He taught in parables not because they were easy to remember but because teaching in parables actually separated those who were His disciples from those who weren't. **"Parables of the Kingdom"** (p. 47) recounts the kingdom significance of some of Jesus' parables.

How would you summarize the main themes of Jesus' teaching?

✝ CHRIST Connection

The Pharisees and scribes criticized Jesus for His practice of welcoming and dining with sinners. The stories Jesus told in response to their criticism focused on God's joy over sinners coming to repentance and illustrated His mission on earth. The God who seeks and saves the lost is Jesus, the Savior whose search and rescue mission is accomplished at great personal cost to Himself.

Parables *of the* Kingdom

The Sower and the Soils (Matt. 13:1-9,18-23; Mark 4:1-9, 13-20; Luke 8:4-8,11-15)	The word about the kingdom—the gospel—is fruitful only in a heart that hears and understands the good news, yet the message must still be shared like the indiscriminate casting of seed on the ground.
The Hidden Treasure and the Priceless Pearl (Matt. 13:44-46)	The kingdom is of such value that it is worth sacrificing everything we have in order to be a part of it.
The Wicked Tenants (Matt. 21:33-46; Mark 12:1-12; Luke 20:9-19)	The kingdom is comprised of people who produce its fruit; failure to produce fruit for God, exemplified in the rejection of His Son, Jesus, is to reject participation in the kingdom of God.
The Good Samaritan (Luke 10:25-37)	The kingdom is comprised of those who see themselves as neighbors without boundaries and who show mercy to others.
The Lost Sheep/Coin/Sons (Luke 15:1-32)	The kingdom of heaven rejoices over a sinner who repents; refusal to rejoice over a sinner's repentance is to find oneself on the outside of the kingdom.
The Pharisee and the Tax Collector (Luke 18:9-14)	The kingdom is comprised of those who humble themselves before God and rely solely upon God's mercy for their salvation; these will be exalted, but those who exalt themselves will be humbled.

Continuing the Discussion

▶ Watch this session's video, and then continue the group discussion using the following guide.

With whom do you identify in Jesus' story of the prodigal sons—the older or younger son? Why?

In what ways is this parable representative of the gospel message?

As a group, read Luke 15:11-13.

Why was the son's request so shocking?

✱ What does the son's request reveal about our sin? What does the father's response reveal about the character of God?

An inheritance is given only after someone dies. When the younger son asked for his share of his father's inheritance, he was declaring that his father might as well be dead—all he cared about was his money. The father would have been dishonored and disgraced by such a request. But the father responds in a way we would not expect. Even though he was surely pained by his son's rejection, he responded with love and grace.

As a group, read Luke 15:17-24.

When was a time in your life that you found yourself in a similar situation as the son?

What are some of the ways the father might have responded to his son coming home?

✱ Where do you see the gospel in his response?

This young man went from the penthouse to the pigpen. He squandered every penny of his inheritance, and so, he set out for home, hoping that his father would take him back as a servant. But that is not what the father did. He took back the young man who had rejected him so coldly and celebrated his return. The father's response is amazing. In this passage, we see the beauty of a father's love, the power of a father's grace, and the joy of a son's return. This is how God treats everyone who comes home. When the lost are found, God rejoices and celebrates. But that doesn't mean everyone shares in His joy.

As a group, read Luke 15:25-32.

> Why is the older son angry? Does his anger surprise you? Why or why not?

✳ What does this interaction with his father reveal about how the older son sees himself?

The older son was just as lost as his younger brother—he just didn't realize it. Where his younger brother was unrighteous, this son was self-righteous. What self-righteous people tend to do is look at the unrighteous and wonder how they could possibly get right with God. But they look at themselves and fail to see why they need to get right with God.

✝ MISSIONAL Application

Record in this space at least one way you will apply the truth of Scripture as one who has experienced the compassion of the loving Father through the gift of Jesus.

Personal Study 1

Selfishness leads to rebelling against the Father's goodness.

Read Luke 15:11-13.

The drama of the three parables in Luke 15 (lost sheep, lost coin, and lost son) is heightened by what had prompted Jesus to tell them. The religious leaders were complaining that Jesus was welcoming sinners at His table. If He were righteous, He would not do that. Jesus did not offer a defense, but instead He shared these three stories.

The first two stories seemed innocent enough. A man loses a sheep, leaves his flock, finds it, and celebrates. A woman loses a coin, sweeps her house, finds it, and celebrates. Jesus' point is that God cares for every lost sinner and that He is seeking them out and celebrates when any are found. But then Jesus begins sharing the third story—a much longer story—and it becomes apparent that Jesus is including some pointed details.

This third story begins with a terrible request. In the culture of Jesus' day, it was normal for sons to assume that upon their father's death, they would receive an inheritance from the family's assets and property. But in Jesus' parable, the younger son demanded his portion prematurely—before the father's death. Today's equivalent would be a teenager spitting in his dad's face and screaming, "I want you dead!" Asking for the inheritance early insinuated that the son couldn't wait for his father to die. He wanted the possessions his father could give him now, even at the expense of their relationship.

A bigger shock follows—the father gave the younger son what he asked for. In fact, he actually gave *both his sons* their inheritance ("to them," v. 12). In those days, the older son would be expected to build a bridge between the father and the younger son and avoid public humiliation. But instead of trying to restore the family's fellowship, the older son silently took his double portion of the fortune. There was neither outcry against the younger brother's action nor passionate defense of the father's honor. The older son pocketed his inheritance, stayed home, and stayed quiet.

Jesus was painting a picture of two types of lost people. The first is openly rebellious—the "in your face" sin of the younger son. The younger son's request epitomizes the enormity and consequence of human sin. "God, we want *what You can give us*, but we don't want *You*!" Consider God's gifts: His beautiful creation, the social order He has established, the institutions of family and government. But just as the younger son wanted to profit from his father without continuing the relationship, we often love these blessings without loving God. We savor the creation and snub the Creator.

Second is a more subtle type of sinner—seen in the older son. He represents someone who appears to be near God but is actually far away. He's the church member who wants God's blessing but could care less about God's name being honored or about being an agent of reconciliation. He doesn't care about his father or his brother—only about himself and what he can get out of the situation.

Jesus' dramatic parable continues with the younger son converting his newly obtained property into cash. When the disgraceful deed was done, the prodigal son headed off to a far country, where he squandered all his wealth in reckless living. The boy wasted his money and life, so when the famine came, he wound up desperate. Jesus described him going and hiring himself out to one of the citizens of that country. The original language uses the phrase "glued himself to" or "joined himself to someone in that country," a description that reveals the son's despair.

Outwardly rebellious sin eventually leads people to squander their lives until they are at the mercy of whatever they have glued themselves to: drugs, alcohol, casinos, sex, music, TV, pornography, relationships, career. We become addicted to something or someone we think will provide hope, but instead, the addiction brings enslavement.

What are some common examples of ways we might squander the good gifts of God?

In what ways does squandering God's gifts lead to slavery instead of freedom?

Personal Study 2

Sorrow leads to relying on the Father's goodness.

Read Luke 15:17-24.

The son had gone to the far country with great aspirations but all he had was soon reduced to nothing. After squandering his inheritance, the son found work for a Gentile. Working for a foreigner was one thing; feeding pigs was another. For a Jew, the pig was the most despised and unclean of animal of them all. Jesus' audience must have bristled at such a terrible picture of this younger son's sin and no doubt agreed with the son's assessment that he was no longer worthy to be a son. But it was in the middle of poverty and disgrace that the young man came to his senses. He remembered that his father was a good man who cared for his servants. He couldn't return to his father as a son, but what about returning as a servant?

Earlier, this son had wished his father were dead. He had publicly humiliated the family's name and honor, sold off his precious inheritance for cash, and deserted the village. He had foolishly squandered all the money and then wound up working for a pagan and craving the food of an unclean animal.

But through it all, the father never stopped loving his child. He never stopped longing to see their relationship restored. He dreamed of them talking, laughing, and spending time together again. Time and time again, his eagerness to see his son drew him to his front yard to stare into the distance looking for his son to return.

Jesus said that on the day when the father saw the son at the edge of the village, he pulled up his robes and ran to him. In Middle Eastern culture, running was considered shameful. An honorable man pulling up his robes and running down the road would be like a father running down Main Street in his pajamas one morning while neighbors watch the spectacle from their porches drinking coffee. It was undignified. Low class. A man of stature never pranced around in public!

Next, the son spoke, and his planned speech took on new meaning. Stunned by his father's unconditional love, the son began to say his prepared words, acknowledging his sin against God and his father and rightly conceding he was unworthy to be a son once more. It was a speech he probably rehearsed many times, but one he never finished.

The son understood his unworthiness to be part of the family and to receive such love. He recognized the weight and depth of his sin and the shame and agony that he had put his father through. But now he was truly repentant! He no longer mentioned his plan to become a hired servant. He realized that the problem was never just about money, the inheritance, and all the squandered belongings. The true issue had always been the broken relationship, which had now been restored due to the father's outrageous display of love and acceptance.

With probably the entire community watching the dramatic events, the father ordered that a robe, shoes, and a signet ring be brought to him. These were signs of acceptance and favor, of a welcoming back into the family. The father wanted his son and everyone else around to know that he and his son were reconciled.

See the heart of God—a father standing on his porch, waiting and watching for his lost child, and when he sees him, he runs toward him, taking the shame of the community upon himself. This is the picture of salvation—God the Son running toward humanity with arms outstretched, not only to embrace us but also to endure public shame and to take the nails reserved for our punishment.

In what ways does the father's treatment of his son go above and beyond what anyone expected?

In what ways does God's treatment of us go beyond what we might hope for?

Personal Study 3

Self-righteousness leads to resenting the Father's goodness.

Read Luke 15:25-32.

The father's embrace and acceptance of his son could have completed Jesus' third and final story. To be parallel with the first two stories, it should have ended there. All three stories would have concluded with joyful celebrations. But Jesus had one more point to make in the final story of this triad. The older brother was lurking in the shadows.

The older son had not been mentioned since the beginning of the parable. The listeners that day might have thought Jesus was establishing him as the positive example—the faithful son. The son who stayed with his father. But that was not Jesus' intention, hinted at earlier when the older son took his share of the inheritance too.

Now, when the older son steps back into the story, we find him not celebrating with his father, but criticizing him. In Jesus' culture, any older son would have been expected to join the feast as quickly as possible. Instead, the older son stayed outside, choosing to murmur about the apparent unfairness of his father's actions. The party was unworthy of his attendance. The son knew he was humiliating his dad, but he didn't care. He became just as rebellious as the prodigal had been at the beginning of the story.

Jesus' parable describes two types of sin—the outward rebellion exposed in the younger son and the inward pride and bitterness concealed in the older son. The gracious father responded to both his children with honor and love. But unlike the younger son, who fell with tears of repentance into his father's arms, the older son simply complained. His boasting about his faithful service revealed more than what is on the surface. He spoke about his father as if he were only a boss to be obeyed, not a father to be loved, and he was convinced he had been treated wrongly.

Notice also how the older son refused to call the younger son his brother. He said, "But when this son of yours came …" If the younger son had to understand repentance as accepting that he was truly his father's son, then the older son had to understand repentance as accepting his younger brother as a true brother! And this is where the Jewish leaders most likely picked up on the point Jesus was making. The younger son represented the "sinners" Jesus was eating with. The older son represented them.

But we can't miss how Jesus ended this parable either. He had just confronted the religious leaders for their pride and bitterness, but his message to them in this story was not one of condemnation, but an offer to repent and experience the Father's love. He wanted his son to come inside so that the family would be whole.

The father then turned the focus away from possessions, works, and obedience. The father desired relationship: "You are always with me!" The issue was neither the faithfulness of the older son nor the reckless living of the younger one. Rather, the spotlight shone on the younger brother not because of anything he had done but because the father-son relationship had been restored.

Jesus ended the parable with a cliffhanger, leaving the audience waiting for the story's resolution: Did the older brother go in and join the family celebration? The answer is left to the listener. You're invited to step up onto the stage and act out the parable's final scene. Will you enter the house of God and become a part of God's family? Or will you stay out in the field, appearing close to God while you are actually far from His heart? Will you remain out in the field, focused on your works and actions without being concerned to have a true relationship with the Father? Won't you come in? Won't you become a part of the reason for celebration? The story's grand finale lies in your hands.

How can our good deeds be a way of walling ourselves off from relationship with God?

Are you more likely to see your Christian life as the drudgery of a servant or a feast for a son? Why?

The Crucifixion of Jesus

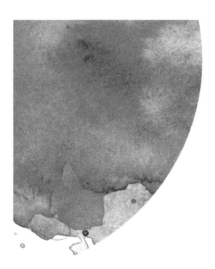

Introducing the Study

Jesus did not come to call the righteous but sinners. He did not come to heal the healthy but the broken. He did not come to the proud but to the humble. Through His ministry, Jesus welcomed those who recognized their need for salvation and who embraced the good news of the kingdom. In word and deed, Jesus showed that the gospel is for all, for all are sinners and all are in need of God's grace.

> **What was your biggest insight through your study of Jesus' parable of the prodigal sons?**

During His three-year ministry, Jesus taught thousands of people, performed numerous miracles, and turned Galilee, Judea, and Samaria upside down. But as impressive as these things were, they are all part of a bigger story—the story of redemption that was driving Jesus to the cross. At the cross, Jesus fulfilled His mission and, in so doing, satisfied the justice of God. It was at the cross where Jesus offered Himself as the punishment for sin and provided the way for humanity to be saved.

> **What thoughts and feelings are raised when you think about Jesus' crucifixion?**

Setting the Context

The cross was never far from the mind of Christ. Throughout His teaching ministry, **Jesus alluded to His death** several times when speaking to His disciples. But His disciples failed to understand what Jesus was telling them. They couldn't understand that Jesus would die, that He needed to die. For them, Jesus was the Messiah who would rule over an earthly kingdom, and to do that, you had to be alive. But that was not Jesus' plan because it was not the Father's plan. Jesus waited on God's timing and plan for when He would be recognized as Lord over heaven and earth.

 Why is the message of the cross foolishness to those who don't believe but a message of power to those who do believe?

After three years of ministry, Jesus approached Jerusalem knowing that He would hang on a cross within the week. Accordingly, He made **final preparations** for what would happen, including fulfilling the Old Testament prophecies of His entrance into Jerusalem, teaching in parables about the end of the age, and preparing for and eating the Passover meal with His disciples.

Meanwhile, **the religious establishment** made their preparations, also according to Scripture, to kill this threat to their power, including paying Judas, one of Jesus' disciples, to betray Him. **"Jesus' Suffering"** (p. 59) recounts the ways Jesus suffered as the climax of His life and ministry, according to the Father's plan.

 Why is it important for Christians to continue to think about and meditate on the crucifixion of Jesus?

✝ CHRIST Connection

Unjustly condemned to death, Jesus willingly took up His cross and suffered the judgment our sins deserve. At the moment He died, the curtain in the temple sanctuary was torn in two, signifying the truth that sinners have access to God through the blood of Christ. The crucifixion of Jesus is the center of history, revealing God's holiness and justice, our sinfulness and unrighteousness, and Christ's humility and love.

Jesus' *Suffering*

Jesus' SUFFERING	Old Testament TYPES and PROPHECIES	Jesus' Followers will SUFFER
Jesus Was Betrayed (Matt. 26:14-16, 47-50; John 13:18-27; Acts 1:16)	• A friend betrays (Ps. 41:9) • 30 pieces of silver as a price (Zech. 11:12-13)	Betrayal by family and friends as those who hate Christ (Luke 21:16-17)
Jesus Felt the Weight of the Cup of God's Wrath (Matt. 26:36-44)	• The cup of the Lord's wrath (Isa. 51:17-20) • The cup of wrath for the nations (Jer. 25:15-29)	**There is no condemnation for those who are in Christ Jesus (Rom. 8:1)**
Jesus Was Mocked, Beaten, and Falsely Accused (Matt. 26:57-68; 27:27-31,39-44)	• The Suffering Servant was despised and rejected, oppressed and afflicted (Isa. 53:3,7) • The psalmist was scorned, despised, and mocked (Ps. 22:6-8)	Suffering and persecution at the hands of the world on account of Jesus' name (Matt. 5:10-11; John 15:20-21; 16:33)
Jesus Was Crucified and Drank the Cup of God's Wrath in Our Place (Matt. 27:33-50; John 19:16-37)	• The Passover (Ex. 11–13), reinstituted in the Lord's Supper—the bread (Jesus' broken body) and the cup of the new covenant (Jesus' shed blood) • The psalmist felt abandoned by God (Ps. 22:1) • The Suffering Servant pierced for others' rebellion (Isa. 53:5) • It pleased the Lord to crush the Servant as an offering of atonement (Isa. 53:10)	**God made Him who had no sin to be sin for us so we might become the righteousness of God in Him (2 Cor. 5:21)**

Continuing the Discussion

 Watch this session's video, and then continue the group discussion using the following guide.

What are some of the ways a non-Christian might view the crucifixion of Jesus?

What are some ways we can combat an over-familiarity and coldness to the story of the cross?

As a group, read Mark 14:22-26.

 How did Jesus give new meaning to the Passover celebration?

As the disciples observed and listened to Jesus at the first Lord's Supper, what do you think might have been going through their minds?

The Passover meal looked back at the exodus and served as a reminder of God's deliverance, love, and power. Jesus added to this meaning by pointing His disciples to look ahead, foreshadowing His death on the cross that would provide a greater deliverance—one from sin and death. Rather than a lamb dying for only one family, Jesus, the Lamb of God, would die for all the world (see John 1:29). Rather than the blood of a lamb covering a door, the bread and wine were symbols of Jesus' body and blood covering whoever trusts in Him. The elements serve as reminders that Jesus sacrificed His body and shed His blood on our behalf to pay for our sins and to make it possible for us to have a relationship with God.

As a group, read Mark 14:32-36.

 How does this garden scene compare with the first garden scene in the Bible—the garden of Eden? What temptations were presented in both?

What was the focus of Jesus' prayers?

Adam and Eve were tempted in Eden to act on their own desires rather than submit to God's will. Jesus was tempted likewise in Gethsemane. But while Adam and Eve succumbed to this temptation, bringing death upon themselves and all of humanity, Jesus acted in obedience. Jesus kept God's will above His own and brought eternal life and salvation to the world.

As a group, read Mark 15:22-41.

> Where do you see Psalm 69:21, Psalm 22:18, and Isaiah 53:12 fulfilled in Mark's account of the crucifixion?

※ Why is it significant that the curtain was ripped, and ripped from top to bottom?

Neither the Father nor Jesus were surprised by the crucifixion. It was known long before. It was planned long before. From our perspective, the cross seemed to be the result of a situation spiraling out of control. But it wasn't. It was the centerpiece of God's design to bring salvation to the world. Jesus' death has once and for all provided access to God's holy presence.

✝ MISSIONAL Application

Record in this space at least one way you will apply the truth of Scripture as a recipient of God's grace through faith in Jesus, the Lamb of God who takes away the sin of the world.

Personal Study 1

Jesus prepares the disciples at the Last Supper.

Read Mark 14:22-26.

For more than a thousand years, God's people were to celebrate the Passover meal to remember the exodus, God's deliverance of His people from bondage in Egypt. But on the night of His betrayal, Jesus added new meaning to this meal. The Passover would no longer only look back at God's deliverance from Egyptian bondage through Moses, but it would also picture God's deliverance from sin's bondage through Christ.

One of the hallmarks of God's law was His requirement that His people offer regular sacrifices. Even before the law was given, God's people intuitively understood the need to sacrifice. But God had a better plan than His people serving Him year after year with sacrifices. He always intended to be the One to offer the ultimate sacrifice for His people. That is why Jesus had come. Not to be served, but to serve. He came "to give his life as a ransom for many" (Mark 10:45).

This was at the center of the new and better covenant God had promised as the Old Testament closed. Jeremiah and Ezekiel both prophesied of a day when hearts of stone would be replaced with hearts of flesh—when God's people would be cleansed of their sin, filled with God's Spirit, and be His people (Jer. 31:31-34; Ezek. 11:19-20; 36:26-36).

This new covenant, this new, one-time sacrifice, was what Jesus had in mind when He spoke of His body being broken and blood poured out during the Last Supper. What the disciples would see on the cross soon after would be the fulfillment of God's promises. No longer would God's people offer goats and bulls for their sin. God was offering Himself.

Then Jesus offered what might have seemed to be an offhand remark, but it was actually a beautiful promise. It was a promise to give His disciples in the room that evening, and us, hope. Jesus would drink the fruit of the vine with them again. It would not be soon, but it would happen, and when it did, they would all be in His Father's kingdom.

The message of the coming kingdom is a message of hope and joy and fulfillment. It is the longing of the Christian heart. This is why we pray, "Your kingdom come" (Matt. 6:10). We anticipate the day when wars and violence cease and when peace reigns. We yearn for the day when sin's teeth have ceased biting and death itself is dead. We hunger and thirst for the kingdom because we hunger and thirst for the King of righteousness, and we will be with Him then and there.

After speaking these words, the disciples and their Teacher headed out into the darkness with singing. Likewise, fueled by the feast of faith and longing for the coming kingdom, we walk through the darkness of the world with hearts inclined to songs of praise for our Savior.

What would it look like for a Christian to yearn for the consummation of the kingdom?

What excites you most about eternity in God's kingdom?

Personal Study 2

Jesus prepares Himself in the garden.

Read Mark 14:32-36.

It was almost time. The cross was only hours away. Jesus knew this and He knew that the cross was God's design. But He also knew that obeying the Father would bring great suffering. So Jesus followed His routine—He found a place to pray.

Jesus wanted to obey the Father. He wanted to bring the Father glory and be the One to bring salvation to the world. And yet, He knew what a Roman crucifixion was like. He understood that the physical agony He would feel would not be His greatest suffering—bearing the sins of the world and being separated from the Father would be. And so, He wrestled with what lay before Him. He was so distressed that He told His disciples He was "deeply grieved to the point of death."

The Bible teaches that those who continue in rebellion to God's Word and refuse to submit to God's will store up wrath for themselves. One way the Bible describes the outpouring of God's wrath is with the imagery of a cup filled with wine, which represents God's wrath or anger (Jer. 25:15-17,28; 49:12). On the day of judgment, God will pour out this wine, and He will make sinners drink every drop until they become drunk with His wrath (Ps. 75:8; Ezek. 23:32-34).

At the cross (the "hour" that Jesus spoke of), God the Father poured out the full cup of His wrath on His own Son as a judgment against sin. Since Jesus took on our sin, He was forsaken and abandoned (Mark 15:34). Anticipating this judgment, Jesus asked His Father, the only One with the authority to remove Him from both *this hour* and *this cup*, if there were any other possible way to bring His will to pass.

But in the end, unlike Adam, Jesus submitted to the Father's will with an emphatic "not what I will, but what you will" (v. 36). Jesus knew that there was no way to fulfill the Father's Word other than by submitting to the Father's will. God would only take this cup away from His people by pouring it out on His righteous Servant (Isa. 51:17,21-22). Jesus received the wounds we deserved, and by faith we receive forgiveness we do not deserve (53:1-12).

Only when we meditate on Christ's life and death are we able to live out our faith. If we fail to ground our efforts to be like Christ in the good news of what Christ has done for us, we will throw up our hands and give up! The cross is what makes our obedience possible. It shapes what our obedience looks like.

This means that like Jesus, we are to submit to the Father's will, even when it results in suffering. We are called to follow Christ, which means we are called to suffer (1 Pet. 2:21). We should not be surprised when suffering comes our way; it is one way God transforms us into the image of His Son. The good news is, though, that by His death and resurrection, Jesus has granted us the power to face any and all suffering we may face (vv. 24-25).

Have you ever submitted to the Father's will knowing it would bring suffering? How does understanding the purposes of God help you face suffering?

How does meditating on Christ help you prepare for suffering? What does a Christ-like response to suffering look like?

Personal Study 3

Jesus lays down His life as the crucified Savior.

Read Mark 15:22-41.

As we read of the events surrounding the crucifixion of Jesus, the word *humiliation* should echo in our minds and hearts. The Son of God was beaten and tortured. Mocked and abused. Insulted and taunted. For over three years, people had gathered around Jesus and looked on in amazement because of what He said and did. Now, the soldiers, religious leaders, and Jews gathered around Jesus and looked on in disgust as the supposed king hung dying on a cross.

Who could endure such ridicule, shame, and torture, especially by choice? At any moment Jesus could have resisted. At any moment He could have fought back. The same mouth that had spoken words to calm a storm could have spoken words to call forth a legion of angels to come to His defense. But Jesus did not do that. He chose, instead, to endure.

And that is why we should also think of the word *humility* as we read this passage. The Son of God demonstrated patience. Love. Grace. Mercy. Jesus humbled Himself and laid down His life for those He had created. The cross is a spectacular drama showing how far the Son of God was willing to go in perfect obedience to His Father, and we are encouraged to live in likewise humility (e.g., Phil. 2:5-11).

The irony in this passage is thicker than blood. The King of kings is mocked by being called a king. He is told to come down and display His glory when doing so would have undone all that He was accomplishing *for* His glory. By saving Himself, He would sacrifice others. But by sacrificing Himself, He would save others. So He stayed on the cross and endured the pain, shame, and wrath, and we are the beneficiaries. The crucified King—a stumbling block to the Jews and foolishness to Gentiles, and yet, the very hope of the world (see 1 Cor. 1:23-25).

Before God spoke light into existence, there was darkness. Before the Israelites' redemption from Egypt, the plague of darkness covered the nation. Now, here at the crucifixion, darkness swallowed the whole land for three hours as a marker of this moment's cosmic significance.

Initial shrieks of terror at the darkness eventually subsided as wonder, fear, and awe overcame the crowd. As light was extinguished, so too was sound. The silence hung heavily like a morning fog until a single cry pierced the stillness: "My God, my God, why have you abandoned me?" (Matt. 27:46).

Some phrases are so embedded in our collective consciousness that they convey much more than the phrase itself: "We hold these truths to be self-evident." "Four score and seven years ago." "I have a dream." "Houston, we have a problem." The same is true of these words uttered from the cross.

Jesus' cry should have resonated in the minds of the onlookers, but they missed His reference. These are the opening words of Psalm 22, a psalm dripping with messianic meaning (see especially vv. 1-2,6-8,12-18). Jesus was not calling upon Elijah, as the crowd supposed. He was identifying Himself as the One to whom the psalm pointed and demonstrating the horror of feeling forsaken by His Father.

And then Jesus let out His last breath. With it, the veil in the temple that separated heaven and earth was split from top to bottom, signifying that this act was accomplished from above.

In the torn curtain, a message is proclaimed. A Son was rejected so that the Father would have many more sons and daughters. The Father forsook His only Son that He might extend forgiveness to a great many children. A Son's sacrifice was accepted in the holy of holies that all who trust in Him might be accepted before the very throne of God.

Why are people prone to miss Jesus' glory on the cross?

If a non-Christian asked you the question, "Why did Jesus die?" how would you respond?

The Resurrection of Jesus

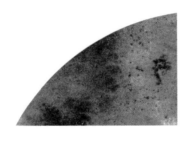
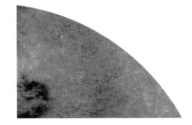
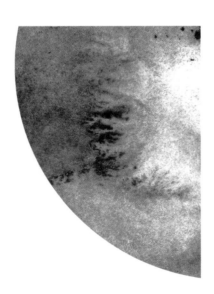
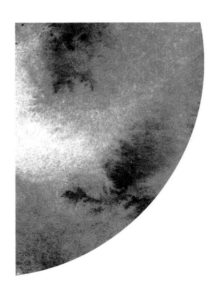

Introducing the Study

Jesus had completed the work the Father had given Him. He had lived and then died, according to His mission. Just as the kingdom of God reverses the principles of this world—where the poor are rich and the mourners are comforted—the death of Jesus brings life to all who believe in Him.

> **How has the death of Jesus been meaningful to you this past week?**

The death of Jesus was not the end; it was a beginning. Though Jesus had died at the hands of the Romans and the Jewish leaders, He had also died according to the plan and purpose of God. But a dead Savior is no Savior at all. Jesus promised to rise from the dead in victory. His followers had given up hope, but God was not finished. Jesus would rise from the dead, validating Jesus' promise of salvation and the rest of God's promises as well.

 How does the resurrection of Jesus validate His promise of salvation through His crucifixion?

Setting the Context

Jesus was crucified on **Good Friday**, and so many of the events and details surrounding His crucifixion fulfilled prophecies, as **"Hearing the Old Testament in Jesus' Crucifixion"** (p. 71) shows. But despite Jesus' repeated warnings of these events, His followers had scattered, worried that they might be next. With evening coming, the Sabbath was about to begin. So Joseph of Arimathea, a wealthy and influential man loyal to Jesus, asked Pilate for Jesus' body and provided a tomb for His **quick burial**, which the faithful women around Jesus prepared.

 What are some specific ways the death of Jesus changes our priorities?

Jesus was dead and in the grave, but **the Jewish leaders** were still nervous. They knew of the prediction that Jesus would rise from the dead, and they were worried that His followers might steal the body and claim He had risen, further perpetuating the notion that Jesus was the Messiah, the Son of God. So the leaders asked Pilate to secure the grave, and the ruler agreed. Pilate assigned **a Roman guard** to the tomb. These soldiers were sure not to let anyone steal Jesus' body.

Jesus was dead. The tomb was secure. And the hearts and hopes of Jesus' followers were crushed as **Easter Sunday** morning crept toward them.

> **What do you think it was like for the followers of Jesus between Good Friday and Easter Sunday?**

✞ CHRIST Connection

On Easter Sunday, God vindicated His Son's perfect sacrifice by raising Him from the dead and beginning the long-promised new creation. Jesus' first followers did not anticipate or believe in the resurrection at first, but the evidence of the resurrection helped grow their faith into full belief. Likewise, through faith, we are united to Christ and share in the promise of being resurrected in His likeness. Sin's curse has been removed, death has been defeated, and we are assured of everlasting life with God.

Hearing the Old Testament *in* Jesus' Crucifixion

OLD TESTAMENT | NEW TESTAMENT

OLD TESTAMENT	NEW TESTAMENT
Passover A Lamb's Blood Was Shed to Cover the Israelites' Doorways (Ex. 11–13)	**The Lord's Supper** Jesus' Blood Was Shed to Cover the People's Sins (Matt. 26:26-29)
The Psalmist Sang of His Suffering at the Hands of Evildoers (Ps. 22:1-18)	**Jesus** Cried Out About His Suffering on the Cross (Matt. 27:35-46)
The Psalmist Sang of the Lord's Protection over the Bones of the Righteous (Ps. 34:19-20)	**Jesus** Not One of His Bones Was Broken (John 19:31-33,36)
The LORD They Will Look at Me Whom They Pierced (Zech. 12:10)	**Jesus** A Soldier Pierced His Side with a Spear, Confirming Death (John 19:33-34,37)
Jonah Three Days and Nights in the Belly of the Fish for His Disobedience (Jonah 1:17)	**Jesus** Three Days and Nights in the Heart of the Earth for Our Salvation (Matt. 12:40)

Continuing the Discussion

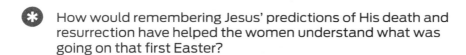 Watch this session's video, and then continue the group discussion using the following guide.

Jesus died for our sins, so why was it essential that He also rise from the dead?

What are some of the ways our perspective on life should change as Christians in light of Jesus' resurrection?

As a group, read Luke 24:1-8.

What are some of the emotions the women might have felt?

✳ How would remembering Jesus' predictions of His death and resurrection have helped the women understand what was going on that first Easter?

With the exception of John, the disciples scattered during Jesus' arrest and crucifixion. They were still in hiding on the Sunday morning after the Sabbath. The women, however, had faithfully stood by during Jesus' agonizing hours on the cross, had helped begin preparing the body for burial, and now were returning to the tomb to finish. They were astonished by what they found—the tomb was open, the guards out of sight, and the body of Jesus gone. Jesus had risen as He had promised, but it would take some time before they and the other followers of Jesus would grasp the implications of this.

As a group, read Luke 24:9-12.

What are some of emotions the disciples might have felt?

Why do you think Peter ran to the tomb?

✳ Why did news of Jesus' resurrection come as a shock to so many people?

Peter had to see it for himself. He had followed Jesus to the high priest's house and denied Christ three times. If Christ were raised, then he could see Christ again and perhaps make up for his mistakes. When he got there, Peter marveled at what he saw. The tomb was indeed empty. He may not have understood it in the early morning light, but surely afterward Peter was able to appreciate what God had allowed him to experience: proof that Christ had risen.

As a group, read Luke 24:13-27.

> Can you relate to these disciples? Have you ever been through an experience only to realize later how God was working in the midst of it?

 What does Jesus' response to the disciples reveal about the nature and message of the Bible?

The two disciples on the road that day knew the facts of what had happened to Jesus, but they failed to make sense of them. They were missing what tied them together. So Jesus used Scripture to show them what they were missing—that all of the Old Testament had pointed to what they witnessed that week. It was all part of God's plan to bring salvation to the world. It was all part of one gospel story. And that is the story the Bible tells, with Jesus as its main character. A thread runs through every book of the Bible pointing to Jesus and His work to redeem God's people, drawing them back to Himself.

✝ MISSIONAL Application

Record in this space at least one way you will apply the truth of Scripture as a believer in the resurrected Christ.

Personal Study 1

The disciples are to remember the promise of a resurrected Savior.

Read Luke 24:1-8.

Imagine what must have been going through the minds of Mary Magdalene, Mary the mother of James, and the others after Jesus was crucified: *What next? Is there any hope? How could this have happened? This was so unjust! We thought He was the Messiah.*

Because work could not be done on the Sabbath, the ladies had to wait until Sunday to attend to Jesus' body. They left their homes early in the morning and made their way to the tomb, stricken with grief. The One they loved was dead. Their hopes for God's kingdom had been dashed. Their teacher was gone.

Everything changed when they arrived at the tomb. The body was gone and grief gave way to confusion. Then they saw two men in "dazzling clothes" and confusion gave way to terror. "Why are you looking for the living among the dead?" they were asked and terror gave way to joy. They realized the truth of Jesus' promise and joy gave way to mission. So the ladies ran off to tell the disciples.

The women rejoiced at the news. Something extraordinary had happened—death had died and Christ was alive! That's why the angels asked, "Why are you looking for the living among the dead?"

The angels helped the women understand by using the words of Jesus from before. Calling the women to remember, the angels said, in effect, "Don't take our word for it, take His! He said to you, 'The Son of Man must be handed over to sinful men, be crucified, and rise again on the third day.'"

The Bible presents a pattern of death following disobedience. Take, for example, Genesis 3 and the sin of Adam and Eve. The next four chapters are marked by death. In Genesis 4, Cain killed Abel. Then Cain feared for his own life (4:14). "Then he died" is the refrain of the genealogy in Genesis 5. Then in Genesis 6–7, death and destruction touched the whole earth as God judged through the flood. Death is an inescapable reality even though God's creation was originally designed for life to flourish.

So what does the resurrection of Jesus mean? Remember the connection between death and disobedience. If death is defeated, our disobedience has been dealt with. Earthly judges condemned Jesus, the innocent One, to the cross. But the Judge of heaven, God Himself, vindicated Jesus by raising Him from the dead. When we trust the verdict of God over the verdict of men, we too are vindicated along with Jesus. His life is our life. His obedience is counted as our own.

How can we understand the meaning of the resurrection—not just *that* it happened but *why* it happened and *what* it means?

What role do the emotions of awe, wonder, and joy play in our sharing the good news of Christ's death and resurrection?

Personal Study 2

The disciples are to believe the evidence of a resurrected Savior.

Read Luke 24:9-12.

"He is not here, but he has risen!" (24:6). That's what the angel had told the women, and the news was almost too good to believe. The women had followed Jesus and supported His ministry. They had watched His torture on the cross. And they had come that morning to anoint Jesus' body only to find a heavenly messenger instead.

How did the women respond to the news of the resurrection? First, they rejoiced. Then, they remembered. Finally, they reported. It would have been understandable for them to stop after the second response and linger at the tomb rejoicing and remembering to prolong the experience. But that's not what they did. The resurrection was a call to action! News like this had to be shared.

Imagine this scenario: Everything happens just as Luke tells it through verse 8—and then nothing else follows. About two weeks later, Peter and John see Mary Magdalene in the market. Peter asks, "Mary, what happened to you after the death of the Lord? Did you ever get to anoint the body?" "Didn't I tell you?" Mary replies. "Jesus rose from the dead that morning!" We can't even fathom the story moving forward in that way. The news of the resurrection is too explosive!

Instead, the women went immediately to find the disciples and share the news with them. But what they found is what we might also find when we report the miracle of the resurrection—skepticism. The disciples knew these women well; they had traveled long miles and hours with them. They were far from strangers, and yet their ravings sounded like nonsense.

These were the disciples who, when they had a chance to stick by their leader and friend, abandoned Him to His death instead. They had scattered like rats when the lights are turned on. Perhaps their doubt came partly from a sense of shame and regret. But, honestly, a resurrection? It was ludicrous. Preposterous. Absolutely unthinkable. So they dismissed the women's claims as delusions of grief.

Or at least most of them did. But these testimonies, far-fetched as they might be, stuck with at least one of the disciples. Something rose up inside Peter—something he hadn't felt in several days. Peter, more than anyone else, knew the shame of betraying Jesus.

He had done it not once, not twice, but three times during Jesus' trials. The hours since then had been absolutely miserable. But the claims of these women? Peter suddenly felt a sense of hope. It wasn't much, but it was there—at least enough to get him moving.

Sometimes it's easy for us to forget that when we share the gospel with others, we are asking them to believe something that is ridiculous. Hilariously impossible even. Surely those who hear today will have the same response as the disciples—just a shake of their heads at the foolishness in front of them. But then there will be those like Peter, who though the message sounded crazy, think that maybe, possibly, crazily, it could be true.

When those people take another step forward, what they will find is the same thing any of us find when we begin to seek the truth of Jesus' resurrection: evidence. Not only the physical evidence of the empty tomb, but eyewitness testimony. Not only eyewitness testimony, but the evidence of lives changed through the risen Christ.

How is your life evidence of the resurrection of Jesus?

How would you respond to someone who claimed the resurrection was ridiculous?

Personal Study 3

The disciples are to recognize the prophecies of a resurrected Savior.

Read Luke 24:13-27.

Luke was a careful historian (see Luke 1:1-4). He was also a remarkable storyteller, as we will see throughout this passage. He begins by introducing two travelers on the seven-mile journey from Jerusalem to a village named Emmaus. The two were disciples of Jesus, but were not part of the Twelve. While they traveled, they discussed the events of the weekend—the arrest, trial, sentencing, and death of Jesus (see v. 20).

And then, a lonely traveler joined them and asked what they were talking about. In verses 15-16, Luke gives us "insider information" that the two travelers did not know—the Man who joined them was Jesus. The passive voice of the verb "were prevented" suggests that someone other than the disciples was responsible for their blindness. But who? Although some suggest Satan, it is much more likely that God was the One who prevented them from recognizing the risen Savior. Jesus looked similar after His resurrection as He did before (the women at the tomb recognized Him). So God supernaturally prevented the eyes of these disciples from recognizing Him. They likely assumed this Man was just another worshiper returning home from Jerusalem.

The two disciples could not believe what the Man had asked. What were they talking about? Was He serious? How could *anyone* not know what had happened in Jerusalem the prior week, especially the last few days? So stunned were the two travelers that they came to a stop. There, in the middle of the road, they stared at Jesus with sadness in their eyes. The two began to rehearse all that had happened concerning Jesus. As you read their account, you will notice that they have the details right. They knew the facts. But you will also notice that they took Jesus on an emotional roller coaster ride: joy, despair, hope, and confusion. Finally, you will notice that they completed their account with a cliffhanger—some had reported that Jesus' body was gone and that an angel said he was alive. They were missing one critical final part of the story—that the report was true! Jesus has risen!

So how did Jesus respond? What did He share with them that they needed to hear? He pointed them back to Scripture—to the revealed plan of God concerning Jesus that had been set in motion from the beginning. The two already had what they were missing. They had the Scriptures that time and time again pointed to what would happen that past weekend. This is why Jesus said that they were "foolish" and "slow."

They didn't need more information; they needed to understand what they already knew—that all of Scripture was one story of the Messiah—the promised Deliverer who would rescue God's people from bondage. Essentially, without drawing attention to Himself just yet, Jesus told Cleopas and the other disciple, "Everything you think you know is actually about Me. That's the key. If you get that, you get the Scriptures. And if you get the Scriptures, you get what happened this past weekend. And if you get what happened this past weekend, you get the resurrection. And if you get the resurrection—and trust in Me—you get eternal life."

For us, that means that everything we read in Scripture must be filtered through the lens Jesus used—Himself and the gospel. Furthermore, God has given us the mission not to present the Bible as a book of virtues or as a moral improvement program, but rather to present the gospel story of the Bible so that others might believe and have eternal life. Our mission is to introduce people to the risen King who has come to redeem, restore, and reconcile people to God.

Our effectiveness in carrying out this mission depends, to a large extent, on how we read the Bible. Do we read it like the Emmaus disciples—collecting information without knowing what to do with it? Or do we read the Bible—all of the Bible—as the testimony to Christ? Do we read and interpret all Scripture in light of Jesus' death and resurrection?

What would you say to someone who argues that the Old Testament Scriptures are no longer relevant for believers today?

How has God used His Word and His people to remind you of Jesus' presence when you have faced distressing situations?

The Commission from Jesus

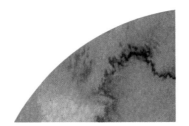
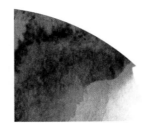
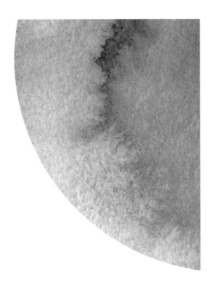

Introducing the Study

The war had been won. Though the resurrection was difficult for Jesus' disciples to believe, they eventually grasped what had happened. Jesus was alive and He had defeated sin and death. They were still afraid of the Jewish leaders and Romans, still coming to terms with what this all meant, but all that Jesus had taught and all that He had done was *beginning* to make sense.

> **What difference should the resurrection of Jesus make in our lives?**

Though the war was over and the ultimate victory won through Jesus' death and resurrection, there was still work to do. Jesus helped the disciples see that they had a significant part to play in God's continuing story. The disciples would become witnesses to the story of Jesus' death and resurrection, continuing God's mission to bless all the nations of the earth.

 How does the resurrection of Jesus serve as a catalyst in sending us out on mission?

Setting the Context

Christ had risen from the dead. He had **appeared to many of His followers** in the days after He came out of the tomb to provide them evidence and encouragement they needed. He appeared to **the women** and **the travelers** on the road to Emmaus.

He appeared to **the disciples** all together in a locked room because they were still living in fear of the Jewish leaders (the locked door was no barrier for Jesus). Because Thomas was not among them and responded with doubt to the other disciples, the scene repeated itself about a week later. **Thomas** no longer doubted but worshiped Jesus—"My Lord and my God!" (John 20:28). He and the disciples had begun to understand Jesus' identity as God.

> How does Jesus' resurrection address our fears and our doubts?

Jesus again appeared to His disciples as they were fishing in the Sea of Galilee. After a miraculous catch of fish, **Peter** swam to the Savior and experienced His grace, love, and forgiveness, being restored after having denied Jesus three times and affirmed for the kingdom mission.

The apostle Paul would later write that Jesus appeared to some **five hundred disciples** at the same time, providing overwhelming reliable testimony to the validity of His resurrection. Jesus was—and is—alive. And He has work for His followers to do—to proclaim the gospel on account of **"Jesus' Exaltation"** (p. 83).

 What role should proclaiming the gospel play in the lives of Jesus' followers?

✝ CHRIST Connection

Before Jesus ascended to the Father, He commissioned His disciples to go into the world and make disciples of all nations. Under the authority of Jesus and with the power of the Holy Spirit, we make disciples of all peoples as we anticipate the return of Christ.

Jesus' *Exaltation*

Jesus' EXALTATION	Respond in FAITH	Respond in WORSHIP and MISSION
The Messiah Was Raised from the Dead (Matt. 28:5-6)	• Blessed are those who believe in Jesus' resurrection, even without seeing Him (John 20:27,29)	• Praise to "my Lord and my God" (John 20:28) • Call people to repentance because one day Jesus will judge the world (Acts 17:30-31)
The Risen King Was Given All Authority in Heaven and on Earth (Matt. 28:18)	• Confess with your mouth that Jesus is Lord and believe in your heart that God raised Him from the dead and you will be saved (Rom. 10:9)	• Go and make disciples of all nations, baptizing them in the name of the Father, Son, and Holy Spirit, and teaching them to observe everything Jesus commanded (Matt. 28:19-20)
The Risen King Ascended into Heaven (Acts 1:9-11; 2:33-36)	• Repent and be baptized in Jesus' name for the forgiveness of sins, and you will receive the promised Holy Spirit (Acts 2:38)	• Set your minds on things above, where Christ is seated (Col. 3:1-17) • Use your gifts from Jesus through the Holy Spirit to serve others (1 Pet. 4:10-11)
Jesus Will Come Again on the Final "Day of the Lord" (Rev. 19–22)	• While doing what is good, entrust yourself to a faithful Creator and Savior (1 Pet. 4:17-19)	• While looking forward to Christ's appearance, proclaim the gospel, endure hardship, do the work of an evangelist, and one day receive from the Lord the crown of righteousness (2 Tim. 4:1-8)

Continuing the Discussion

Watch this session's video, and then continue the group discussion using the following guide.

Why do you think Jesus appeared to so many people after His resurrection?

How does Jesus' resurrection from the dead impact our mission to tell the world about His crucifixion for the sin of the world?

As a group, read Matthew 28:16-20.

Why did Jesus begin His commission with a statement of His authority?

What are the key parts of Jesus' commission?

How do worship and mission relate to one another?

Jesus first reminds us that everything He commands is through the authority He was given by God the Father. Each one of these commands is an important component of the Great Commission: go; make disciples; baptize; teach; and remember His presence. If we remove any one of these, reaching all nations with the gospel of Christ is compromised. Each and every believer and church shares in the responsibility and privilege of taking the good news of Jesus to the world.

As a group, read Acts 1:4-8.

Why was it essential for the disciples to wait for the Holy Spirit before embarking on the mission Jesus had given?

What does it mean to be Jesus' witness? What are we witnesses to?

Jesus had given His followers a mission, and that mission was essential. But they lacked one thing that was essential to complete that mission—power. They would not be able to fulfill it. They needed power from outside of themselves, power from God. That is why they needed to wait for the Holy Spirit. Without the Spirit, there is no power. The Spirit is the energy that enables believers to overcome their fears and to fulfill what their Master has commanded them to do—to be His witnesses. A witness is someone who has seen or experienced something and then tells others about it. In Christianity, a witness is someone who has experienced Jesus Christ through the gospel and then tells the unbelieving world about Him.

As a group, read Acts 1:9-11.

 What was the significance of Jesus' ascension into heaven?

What does this teach us about Christ's future coming?

The angels confirmed that Jesus, who was taken from them, would come back in the same way: visibly, bodily, and with the clouds of glory. For now, Jesus was returning to the place of glory He had left next to the Father. But although Jesus was gone, the disciples were to be busy with His commission. This was a mandate for all, including believers today, to stop gazing and get to work being on mission with God.

✝ MISSIONAL Application

Record in this space at least one way you will apply the truth of Scripture as a disciple of Jesus who will obey His Great Commission in the power of the Holy Spirit.

Personal Study 1

Jesus' disciples are to make disciples of all the nations.

Read Matthew 28:16-20.

The Savior had risen from the grave. Death had been conquered. And now the King of kings was ready to give instructions to His disciples. The anticipation of seeing the resurrected Jesus must have been palpable. But at the same time, we know the disciples were still struggling to understand what Jesus' death and resurrection meant. And so, here they were heading to Galilee to see the One they had been waiting for, the One that not too long ago they thought had been lost forever. When they saw Him, they worshiped, but some doubted.

Jesus wasn't shaken by their unbelief, nor was He discouraged by their slowness to grasp what His resurrection meant. They would understand soon enough; God was sending them something, or better yet Someone, to help them with that. But for now, Jesus continued advancing the mission He had been given from the Father—a mission He was now sharing with His followers. But before He could send His disciples on this mission—before He could share His commission with them—He needed to establish the authority and power behind it—Himself.

It was as important for Jesus' disciples to understand His preeminence over all things that day as it is for us to understand it today. The reality of His power and authority didn't end with His resurrection or ascension, nor at the writing of the biblical text. His kingdom and His authority are eternal.

Since Jesus has authority over all the earth, He therefore commands the disciples to go to all nations. Every tribe, tongue, and nation is under the authority of Jesus and within His gaze seeking the lost. So, we go; but where?

Are we to "go" to a foreign land or to our neighbor across the street? Jesus didn't say. But we do know that the call to make disciples is a call to action. And there's no mistake that Jesus would say "all nations." *All* encompasses *every* place on this earth. Jesus wants no stone unturned, no land to be barren of His name. His desire is for the gospel to be proclaimed to the ends of the earth.

The disciples were commanded to go and make other disciples. By its biblical definition, a *disciple* is a follower of Jesus, someone who learns from Him to live like Him. So, these followers of Jesus were to go and find other people to become followers of Jesus.

Once we have proclaimed the good news to people, and once at least some of those people have placed their faith and trust in the finished work of Jesus on the cross, Jesus commands us then to baptize these new disciples in the name of the Father, the Son, and the Holy Spirit. Baptism is the faithful display of that saving work of Jesus. It is a proclamation of the work that has been done in the believer's heart, which shouts to an unbelieving world that Hope has come. It is an outward sign of the inward transformation of the believer—a move from death (to sin) to life (in Jesus).

But we see in Matthew 28:20 that this isn't the end of the work. Once again, Jesus didn't shy away from the use of the word "all." Jesus told the disciples that they were to teach these new believers all the things Jesus had commanded so they could, in turn, obey their Savior. On their own, this would be another daunting task, but we know that Jesus has given them this instruction in light of His own authority and power.

At the conclusion of His commission, Jesus lovingly reminded the disciples (and us) that they will not be alone in their mission: "And remember, I am with you always, to the end of the age." What began with a declaration of His power and authority ends with the declaration of His faithful presence even to the end of time and then forevermore.

What fears do you have that would keep you from obeying the mission Jesus has given to us?

How does the reality of Jesus' authority over all of heaven and earth overcome those fears?

Personal Study 2

Jesus' disciples are to be His witnesses through the Spirit's power.

Read Acts 1:4-8.

Between Jesus' resurrection and ascension into heaven, He prepared the disciples for their ministry in His name. He ordered them to wait in Jerusalem for the promise of the Father to come (Acts 1:4).

But what was this promise? Jesus had already been crucified as the perfect sacrifice for sins, and in being raised from the dead, He had dealt sin its death blow. Furthermore, He had already commissioned His followers and strengthened and encouraged them for the mission ahead with His many appearances and conversations. So what was the promise of the Father that remained?

The Father had promised a baptism that couldn't come from a man. In Luke 3:15-17, John the Baptist recognized the divine authority and supremacy of Jesus, the One coming after him. This Jesus wasn't a mere man, and He had power and authority far beyond his own. So much so that John didn't even consider himself worthy to untie the sandals on Jesus' feet—he didn't feel worthy to perform the lowest duty of a slave for Jesus.

Now, Jesus tells His disciples that they would receive the gift of the Third Person of the Trinity—the Holy Spirit. This is the Father's remarkable promise, the baptism of the Holy Spirit, a baptism that would define their identity as the followers of Jesus.

The baptism of the Holy Spirit occurred at Pentecost, which takes place in Acts 2. At that time, the believers would be filled with the Holy Spirit and be given power to proclaim the gospel. They would be given the supernatural gift to speak in various languages for the benefit of so many Jews and Gentile converts who had come for the festival from various nations speaking various languages (Acts 2:1-11). This was the promised power and gift awaiting them—the Holy Spirit, the fuel for obeying the Great Commission.

Jesus told the disciples they would receive power when the Holy Spirit came upon them—when He baptized them with the Holy Spirit. This isn't just any power, it's power from the Third Person of the Trinity, the power of God. The Holy Spirit helps Christians as they strive for holiness, obedience, and faithfulness to Jesus' mission.

But one way that the disciples were about to experience the Spirit, and one that every Christian experiences, was His enabling power to speak and proclaim the gospel.

Jesus had shared similar words in Luke 24: "And look, I am sending you what my Father promised. As for you, stay in the city until you are empowered from on high" (v. 49). What encouragement the disciples must have felt knowing they would receive power to complete the Great Commission that was just issued to them days before. Surely they were grateful to know that they wouldn't need to go out and make disciples of all nations in their own strength and with their own wisdom. Instead, they would be guided and empowered by the Holy Spirit, who would give them the comfort, courage, and strength they would need for this mission.

Jesus redirected their attention to the task at hand—it was a time for mission. They were not going to proclaim the gospel in Judea alone; they were going to share about Jesus in Jerusalem, Judea, Samaria, and, if the mission wasn't clear enough, "to the end of the earth" (Acts 1:8). This was an impossible mission for the first disciples on their own, but think of how comforting for them it must have been to know they weren't going alone. Jesus had promised to be with them, and He would be, not physically but spiritually through the promise of the Father. They were going with and in the power of the Holy Spirit. And isn't it comforting for us to know that our mission to share the gospel of Jesus isn't done alone either?

Why are we prone to overlook the gift and ministry of the Holy Spirit?

What are some examples of the Holy Spirit's power you have seen in Scripture?

Personal Study 3

Jesus' disciples are to anticipate His return.

Read Acts 1:9-11.

After Jesus encouraged His disciples to wait for the Father's promised gift and prophesied about the spread of the gospel to the end of the earth, He was taken up in a cloud to heaven. What a privilege it was for the disciples to watch the ascension. And in God's kindness to them, they were reminded once again that the Father was with them, that His promises are true, and that Jesus would come again just as He had left. Jesus departed in a cloud, and He will return on the clouds of heaven.

The angels' comforting statement to the disciples also pointed to the form in which Jesus ascended. He ascended in bodily form, scars and all, and He will return as a man coming for His bride, the church.

Remarkably the God-man will remain fully God and fully man for eternity. He didn't shed His skin upon His return to heaven. Even as He is interceding for us at the right hand of the Father, it is as a man. He continues to relate to us in a glorified state. He had the power to be rid of that body, but in His great love and care for us, He has chosen to be like us in every way, except without sin, for all eternity (Heb. 2:17-18; 4:15). And after Jesus' ascension, the angels assured the disciples that Jesus would return again, in the same form.

We know this to be true of Jesus upon His return to heaven: He is at the right hand of the Father exercising the authority that was and is and always will be His as God, and that authority He received as the once-humiliated, forever-exalted Messiah. Paul proclaimed Jesus' authority in this poetic praise in Colossians 1:15-20:

> He is the image of the invisible God, the firstborn over all creation. For everything was created by him, in heaven and on earth, the visible and the invisible, whether thrones or dominions or rulers or authorities—all things have been created through him and for him. He is before all things, and by him all things hold together. He is also the head of the body, the church; he is the beginning, the firstborn from the dead, so that he might come to have first place in everything. For God was pleased to have all his fullness dwell in him, and through him to reconcile everything to himself, whether things on earth or things in heaven, by making peace through his blood, shed on the cross.

It is this Christ who is seated at the Father's right hand interceding for His disciples with full knowledge of their weaknesses and frailties. Christ has all authority for all eternity. As the God-man, He is the only One able to stand between sinful humanity and holy God and bring the two together. He is the only One who is able to save those who come to the Father through Him, both now and forevermore (Heb. 7:25). So we can share the gospel of this Savior-King with full assurance that He is reigning even now and that He still saves those who believe.

As we live out the mission Jesus gave to His disciples, we can do so with confidence and anticipation. We can look forward to the day when Jesus will return. And when He does come again, no one will mistake His identity. The authority that Jesus now has in heaven and earth will be clear. He will exercise that authority to make all things right.

How does knowing Jesus will return motivate you to live out the mission He has given us?

How do you think it would change your daily perspective if you spent time thinking about the return of Jesus every day?

Tips for Leading a Small Group

Follow these guidelines to prepare for each group session.

Prayerfully Prepare

Review
Review the weekly material and group questions ahead of time.

Pray
Be intentional about praying for each person in the group. Ask the Holy Spirit to work through you and the group discussion as you point to Jesus each week through God's Word.

Minimize Distractions

Create a comfortable environment. If group members are uncomfortable, they'll be distracted and therefore not engaged in the group experience. Plan ahead by considering these details:

Seating

Temperature

Lighting

Food or Drink

Surrounding Noise

General Cleanliness

At best, thoughtfulness and hospitality show guests and group members they're welcome and valued in whatever environment you choose to gather. At worst, people may never notice your effort, but they're also not distracted. Do everything in your ability to help people focus on what's most important: connecting with God, with the Bible, and with one another.

Include Others

Your goal is to foster a community in which people are welcome just as they are but encouraged to grow spiritually. Always be aware of opportunities to include any people who visit the group and to invite new people to join your group. An inexpensive way to make first-time guests feel welcome or to invite someone to get involved is to give them their own copies of this Bible study book.

Encourage Discussion

A good small-group experience has the following characteristics.

Everyone Participates
Encourage everyone to ask questions, share responses, or read aloud.

No One Dominates—Not Even the Leader
Be sure that your time speaking as a leader takes up less than half of your time together as a group. Politely guide discussion if anyone dominates.

Nobody Is Rushed Through Questions
Don't feel that a moment of silence is a bad thing. People often need time to think about their responses to questions they've just heard or to gain courage to share what God is stirring in their hearts.

Input Is Affirmed and Followed Up
Make sure you point out something true or helpful in a response. Don't just move on. Build community with follow-up questions, asking how other people have experienced similar things or how a truth has shaped their understanding of God and the Scripture you're studying. People are less likely to speak up if they fear that you don't actually want to hear their answers or that you're looking for only a certain answer.

God and His Word Are Central
Opinions and experiences can be helpful, but God has given us the truth. Trust God's Word to be the authority and God's Spirit to work in people's lives. You can't change anyone, but God can. Continually point people to the Word and to active steps of faith.

How to Use the Leader Guide

Prepare to Lead

Each session of the Leader Guide is designed to be **torn out** so you, the leader, can have this front-and-back page with you as you lead your group through the session.

Watch the session teaching video and **read through the session content** with the Leader Guide tear-out in hand and notice how it supplements each section of the study.

Use the **Session Objective** in the Leader Guide to help focus your preparation and leadership in the group session.

Questions and Answers

✳ Questions in the session content with **this icon** have some sample answers provided in the Leader Guide, if needed, to help you jump-start the conversation or steer the conversation.

Setting the Context

This section of the session always has an **infographic** on the opposite page. The Leader Guide provides an activity to help your group members interact with the content communicated through the infographic.

MISSIONAL Application

The Leader Guide provides a **MISSIONAL Application statement** about how Christians should respond to the truth of God's Word. Read this statement to the group and then direct them to record in the blank space provided in their book at least one way they will respond on a personal level, remembering that all of Scripture points to the gospel of Jesus Christ.

Pray

Conclude each group session with a prayer. **A brief sample prayer** is provided at the end of each Leader Guide tear-out.

Session 1 · Leader Guide

Session Objective
Show that the birth of Jesus was a fulfillment of what the Old Testament pointed to and that He is the One whom Israel and the world have waited for.

Introducing the Study
Use these answers as needed for the question highlighted in this section.

- They may not have noticed or cared.
- They may have experienced questions and doubts regarding God's care for them.
- They may have been angry and felt abandoned by God.

Setting the Context
Use these answers as needed for the question highlighted in this section.

- So we see the coming of Jesus as God's Plan A for the world, not a Plan B.
- So we understand the meaning of Jesus' birth according to God's intent and not just our own imaginative ideas.
- So we recognize who Jesus is and why He came.

Use the following activity to help group members see the significance of a Christ-centered reading of Scripture.

Encourage group members to look through the connections on **"Hearing the Old Testament in Jesus' Birth"** (p. 11). Then ask the following questions: "Which fulfillment of Old Testament prophecy stands out to you the most? Why?" "Why does it matter that Jesus came as a descendant of Abraham and David?" "What is significant about prophecies regarding Jesus being delivered during the times of the prophets and kings?"

Read this paragraph to transition to the next part of the study.

The Bible, from first to last, is the story of God's work in the world, and His work has always been centered on the person and work of Jesus Christ, God's Son. Our study of the Old Testament up to this point has been pointing to and preparing the way for the coming of Jesus so that we will recognize Him and believe in Him for eternal life.

Continuing the Discussion

Watch this session's video, and then as part of the group discussion, use these answers as needed for the questions highlighted in this section.

Luke 1:26-33

- So we know for certain Jesus was the One God sent to save us from our sin.
- So we can proclaim to the world the truth about Jesus with confidence and boldness.
- So we can again see that God is indeed the promise-keeping God He has always been.

Luke 1:51-55

- God promised Abraham an offspring through whom would come the blessing to the world; Jesus is that offspring.
- The promised land to Abraham and his descendants will find its ultimate fulfillment in the worldwide and eternal reign of Jesus as King over His people.
- God promised to bless Abraham and his descendants; Jesus is the ultimate blessing for God's people.

Luke 2:4-7

- Being born in the city of David, Jesus was to fulfill God's promise to David of an eternal king.
- Jesus' humble birthplace meant He would identify with the poor, the lowly, and the humble and bring salvation to all who humble themselves.
- Jesus did not come to be served but to serve others; He came not in pride but in humility.

Share the following statement with the group. Then direct them to record in the space provided in their book at least one way they will apply the truth of Scripture as one who believes in and follows after our humble Savior and King.

✚ MISSIONAL Application

Because Jesus' humility brought about our salvation, we trust God's plan for our lives as we humbly and joyfully introduce others to Jesus, our Savior and King.

Close your group in prayer, thanking God for His willingness to humble Himself in Christ to come to us.

Session 2 · Leader Guide

Session Objective

Show that God prepared Jesus for His earthly ministry through John the Baptist's ministry as a messenger and also through His baptism and temptation in the wilderness. Where Adam and Israel failed, Jesus succeeded, proving He is the sinless Savior we need.

Introducing the Study

Use these answers as needed for the question highlighted in this section.

- Humility should be a defining characteristic of a follower of Jesus.
- Showing care in the name of Jesus for the poor and the outcast exemplifies the character of the Savior we serve.
- Jesus set aside His privileges as the glorified Son of God for His mission to seek and save the lost, so we must also sacrifice our privileges for the mission.

Setting the Context

Use these answers as needed for the question highlighted in this section.

- Jesus' early years are not the main focus of Jesus' gospel mission.
- It is possible they were very ordinary as Jesus grew up as a human boy.
- No explicit prophecies regarding Jesus' childhood that needed to be fulfilled.

Use the following activity to help group members see the importance of Jesus' being both fully God and fully man.

Call attention to **"Jesus Is God"** (p. 23) and ask group members to identify the points related to Jesus' childhood. Then encourage them to marvel at the thought of the preexistent Son of God taking on flesh and living as a little child within His creation. Ask the following questions: "What are some questions raised by the Son of God taking on flesh?" "What might it mean that Scripture does not tease out for us all the implications of Jesus' deity and humanity?" "How does Jesus' being fully human teach us about what it means to be a human being made in the image of God?"

Read this paragraph to transition to the next part of the study.

The divine and human natures of Jesus are vitally important for the work that He came to earth to do, and the preparation of Jesus in His baptism and wilderness temptation reflect the significance of His two natures. We must never forget that Jesus is both fully God and fully man.

Continuing the Discussion

Watch this session's video, and then as part of the group discussion, use these answers as needed for the questions highlighted in this section.

Mark 1:1-8

- Repentance is changing your mind about your sin; what you once desired to do as a violation of God's law you now reject in favor of doing what God wants you to do.
- Repentance is changing the direction of your life; heading down the broad road leading to destruction, repenting means turning around and following the narrow path of Jesus that leads to life.

Mark 1:9-11

- Jesus came to be like us in every way, except without sin, so He was baptized in order to identify Himself with the repentant sinners He came to save.
- Jesus' baptism affirmed the ministry and message of John the Baptist.
- Jesus' baptism was a step of obedience to God the Father, as demonstrated by His affirmation of Jesus from the heavens.

Matthew 4:1-11

- They were both tempted regarding food.
- They were both tempted regarding the nature of deity.
- Adam and Eve doubted God's word, whereas Jesus trusted in God's word completely, even using it as a weapon of defense against Satan's temptations.

Share the following statement with the group. Then direct them to record in the space provided in their book at least one way they will apply the truth of Scripture as a repentant believer in Christ who will follow the leading of the Holy Spirit.

MISSIONAL Application

Because the Spirit of God lives in us and we have been credited with Christ's perfect righteousness, we resist temptation by resting in our identity in Christ, the One who overcame temptation in our place.

Close your group in prayer, thanking God that His Word is trustworthy and true.

Session 3 · Leader Guide

Session Objective

Show that all of Jesus' miracles were designed to reveal His identity and support His teachings, as they also flowed from His deep compassion for people.

Introducing the Study

Use these answers as needed for the question highlighted in this section.

- God's Word is a weapon for defeating temptation, so we need to know it in order to wield it.
- With a sinful heart and motive, God's Word can be used to justify our sinful actions.
- God's Word teaches us about who God is and how we should live in this world.

Setting the Context

Use these answers as needed for the question highlighted in this section.

- Success in faithfully fending off temptation can embolden your faith and obedience.
- He experienced want in the desert according to the leading of the Spirit, and after the time and temptation, the Lord provided for His needs, reaffirming trust in God's will.
- He experienced firsthand as a human being that God's Word accomplishes its purposes, so He is worth obeying.

Use the following activity to help group members see the purpose of Jesus' miracles.

Ask group members to name some signs they see on a regular basis *(signs for businesses; billboards; traffic signs; etc.)*. Then ask what is the purpose of these signs *(to get attention; to draw you in; to provide direction and instruction)*. Let group members review the seven miracles on **"Jesus' Signs in the Gospel of John"** (p. 35) and ask the following questions: "Why do you think John chose to call these miracles signs?" "How do the various responses to Jesus' signs relate to the responses people have to signs in our day?" Conclude this activity by reading John 20:30-31, which gives John's reason for recording these signs in his Gospel: "Jesus performed many other signs in the presence of his disciples that are not written in this book. But these are written so that you may believe that Jesus is the Messiah, the Son of God, and that by believing you may have life in his name."

Continuing the Discussion

Watch this session's video, and then as part of the group discussion, use these answers as needed for the questions highlighted in this section.

Mark 1:21-28

- They supported the power of His gospel message and teaching.
- They confirmed His authority over both the physical and spiritual realms.
- They validated His ministry as the promised Messiah.

Mark 1:35-38

- Jesus was not concerned with popularity or fame; these were not integral to His mission.
- Jesus' mission was not primarily about miracles but about the message of repentance and faith.
- Jesus wanted as many people as possible to hear the gospel message.

Mark 1:39-42

- It is powerful to consider that the God of all the universe is moved with compassion by the plight of His image bearers and their faith.
- Jesus is the image of God, the full revelation of God's character, and this scene of Jesus' compassion and miracle-working power combats the way the world often sees God.
- Touching a leper made one unclean, but in this case, the purity of Jesus went the other way and washed this leper clean of his uncleanness.

Share the following statement with the group. Then direct them to record in the space provided in their book at least one way they will apply the truth of Scripture as one who has experienced Jesus' power and compassion in salvation from sin.

MISSIONAL Application

Because we have experienced the authority, power, and love of Christ in our salvation, we share Jesus with others with compassion for them today and concern for them for eternity.

Close your group in prayer, thanking God that Jesus is not put off by our sin but in His compassion is willing to come near to us.

Session 4 · Leader Guide

Session Objective

Show from this parable that Jesus came to bring all kinds of sinners to repentance and that His teachings all centered on this purpose—how we can be right with God through Him.

Introducing the Study

Use these answers as needed for the question highlighted in this section.

- Unexpected characters by nature catch you off guard and force you to reckon with their purpose.
- Unexpected characters can challenge your routine patterns of thinking.
- We most often identify with protagonists in stories, so unexpected characters cause us to rethink our perceptions of people and even our understanding of God's ways.

Setting the Context

Use these answers as needed for the question highlighted in this section.

- Words and deeds are meant to back each other up—walk the walk and talk the talk.
- Good deeds can be undermined or seen for the selfish actions they are because of the way one might talk about them.
- We should reject the pattern that says, "Do as I say, not as I do."

Use the following activity to help group members see the spiritual aspect of Jesus' parables.

Ask group members what some of their favorite stories are and what they have meant to them. Explain that we find meaning in stories because that is how God made us, but understanding the proper spiritual significance of Jesus' parables apart from faith in Him is impossible because true understanding leads to faith-filled response— it leads to repentance and faith and obedience.

Allow group members to look over the information on **"Parables of the Kingdom"** (p. 47). Then ask the following questions: "What are some ways Christians need to respond to the parables Jesus told about the kingdom of God?" "How are these responses different from the ways of this world?"

Continuing the Discussion

Watch this session's video, and then as part of the group discussion, use these answers as needed for the questions highlighted in this section.

Luke 15:11-13

- Sin is an offense to the character and honor of God.
- Sin is selfish, self-centered, and self-pleasing.
- God is gracious and patient.

Luke 15:17-24

- Heaven celebrates when even one sinner repents of his or her sin (Luke 15:7,10).
- God's gift of salvation takes an enemy of God and creates a son or daughter of God.
- God does not keep a record of wrongs with His children but welcomes them home when they repent and return to Him.

Luke 15:25-32

- The older brother sees himself as a slave of the father, working to earn his good favor.
- The older son sees himself as righteous and worthy because he is better than his brother.
- He sees himself as a dutiful and obedient son.

Share the following statement with the group. Then direct them to record in the space provided in their book at least one way they will apply the truth of Scripture as one who has experienced the compassion of the loving Father through the gift of His Son, Jesus.

MISSIONAL Application

Because we have been sought and saved by God and experienced His salvation in Jesus, we are quick to celebrate the Father's goodness in welcoming any repentant sinner home.

Close your group in prayer, thanking God that He always welcomes us with open arms of forgiveness when we repent of our sin and turn to Him in faith.

Session 5 · Leader Guide

Session Objective

Show that the crucifixion is the apex of the story of Scripture and that only through Jesus' death can we be saved from our sin.

Setting the Context

Use these answers as needed for the questions highlighted in this section.

- It makes no earthly sense for the Savior, God's Son, to die for human beings.
- By nature, we expect displays of power from those we want to worship, not sacrifice.
- To those who do believe, the cross of Jesus is beautiful because it is there that our sin problem is dealt its deathblow as Jesus dies in our place to save us from sin and death.

- Christians never move beyond the gospel of Jesus' death and resurrection because it is the power of God for both salvation and sanctification.
- So we remember that the remedy for our sin is also the remedy for the sin of the whole world.
- So we can see the beautiful example of Jesus laying down His life for us and follow in His steps as we love and serve others with the gospel in Jesus' name.

Use the following activity to help group members see what the crucifixion means for the followers of Jesus.

Encourage group members to read over **"Jesus' Suffering"** (p. 59) and to feel the weight of the suffering Jesus experienced for our sake. Ask the group to identify what distinguishes the red and blue rows. Use the following to help explain the differences.

- **Red Rows:** Jesus' physical suffering at the hands of human beings. Those who are Jesus' disciples are expected to take up their cross of suffering and follow Him, even though that may mean betrayal, physical suffering, and even death for the sake of Jesus' name.

- **Blue Rows:** Jesus' experience of suffering the wrath of God against sin. While Jesus' followers should expect suffering at the hands of human beings, they will ***never suffer the wrath of God*** because Jesus has taken that in their place to save them from sin and its eternal consequences.

Ask the following question: "How do the blue rows encourage you, even with the expectation of suffering found in the red rows?"

Continuing the Discussion

Watch this session's video, and then as part of the group discussion, use these answers as needed for the questions highlighted in this section.

Mark 14:22-26

- The Lord's Supper superseded the Passover meal as a remembrance of the greater exodus for God's people from slavery to sin.
- The blood of the Passover lamb pointed forward to the blood of Jesus.
- The Passover was celebrated by families, but the Lord's Supper is celebrated by churches comprised of people from every tribe, language, and nation.

Mark 14:32-36

- Adam and Eve succumbed to their temptation, but Jesus struggled mightily against temptation and prevailed.
- Adam and Eve desired to be like God, but Jesus, who is God, humbled Himself to obey the Father and die for humanity.
- Adam's sin brought death upon humanity; according to God's will, Jesus resolved to take that death upon Himself in order to bring life to humanity.

Mark 15:22-41

- The curtain barred access to the most holy place, where God was said to dwell in the temple in His holiness.
- The curtain was ripped from top to bottom, indicating that this was the work of God opening up access to His presence through the death of Jesus.
- No longer was the most holy place restricted to the high priest, but now God's holy presence is available to all because of Jesus' sacrifice.

Share the following statement with the group. Then direct them to record in the space provided in their book at least one way they will apply the truth of Scripture as a recipient of God's grace through faith in Jesus, the Lamb of God.

✝ MISSIONAL Application

Because we have been forgiven of our sins and given Christ's righteousness, we seek to proclaim not only that Jesus died on the cross but why He died.

Close your group in prayer, praising God for providing Jesus as a sacrifice for our sins and thanking Him for the freedom that comes through that sacrifice.

Session 6 · Leader Guide

Session Objective

Show that the resurrection was difficult for the first disciples to believe, but they had been given all they needed—both prophecy and proof—to recognize that Jesus was crucified and raised again on the third day.

Introducing the Study

Use these answers as needed for the question highlighted in this section.

- Jesus said He would rise from the dead, so if He didn't, then He would be a liar and could not be our perfect Savior.
- To be our Savior, Jesus needed to defeat both sin and death. Jesus' resurrection shows He has indeed beaten death; therefore, He has defeated sin for us.
- It fulfills Old Testament prophecies that the Messiah would suffer for sin and be restored to the living.

Setting the Context

Use these answers as needed for the question highlighted in this section.

- The death of Jesus frees us from slavery to sin, so our priorities now begin to shift from gratifying self to honoring God and serving others.
- Jesus' death has saved us, so we lay down our lives to serve Him in love.
- Since we have been saved by the death of Jesus, we now live to proclaim the message of a crucified Savior for all the world to believe and give Him glory.

Use the following activity to help group members see how Jesus' crucifixion and resurrection relate to one another.

Direct group members to look at the connections on **"Hearing the Old Testament in Jesus' Crucifixion"** (p. 71). Then ask the following questions: "Why do you think there are so many explicit prophecies relating to Jesus' crucifixion?" "What is the relationship between Jesus' crucifixion and resurrection? Is one more important than the other? Why or why not?"

Explain that regarding Jesus' crucifixion and resurrection, we cannot have one without the other—they are both equally and vitally important. The crucifixion of Jesus would mean nothing without His resurrection; we would still be dead in our sins. And there is certainly no need for a resurrection if Jesus was not crucified, in which case we are also still dead in our sins. We believe in and serve a crucified and risen Savior. Anything less is not the Jesus of the Bible.

Continuing the Discussion

Watch this session's video, and then as part of the group discussion, use these answers as needed for the questions highlighted in this section.

Luke 24:1-8

- Jesus said He would be crucified and He was—He always spoke the truth.
- Because Jesus predicted His crucifixion, He could also be believed in His prediction of His resurrection.
- Jesus' predictions would have recalled the words of the prophets that addressed the suffering and resurrection of the Messiah.

Luke 24:9-12

- It sounded like nonsense; yes, He raised others from the dead, but could He Himself rise when He was dead?
- Because they failed to believe all that the Scriptures had said regarding the Messiah.
- Because our sinful hearts make it hard to believe God can do the impossible.

Luke 24:13-27

- The Bible is clear that the Messiah would suffer and rise again.
- Though the books of the Bible have been written by numerous authors, there is one Author—God Himself—who has inspired every word so the whole story points to Jesus.
- In our sin, we miss the point of Scripture; only with the wisdom of God through the Holy Spirit can we rightly discern Scripture and obey it.

Share the following statement with the group. Then direct them to record in the space provided in their book at least one way they will apply the truth of Scripture as a believer in the resurrected Christ.

✛ MISSIONAL Application

Because we have experienced the reality of the resurrection and its power in bringing us new life in Christ, we go and tell others the good news of Christ's victory over sin and death, calling people to trust in Jesus and receive resurrection life.

Close your group in prayer, thanking God for the unique hope we have as Christians because of the resurrection of Jesus.

Session 7 · Leader Guide

Session Objective

Show that Jesus gave His followers clear instructions for how they were to make disciples of all the nations through the power of the Holy Spirit as they work and wait for His return.

Introducing the Study

Use these answers as needed for the question highlighted in this section.

- God has done the impossible in our minds and raised Jesus from the dead; how can we not go out and tell others about what He has done?
- The power that raised Jesus from the dead now lives in us, empowering us for the gospel mission.
- Because Jesus has been raised, we have confidence in our own resurrection, so we can face down any threat with boldness as we share the gospel with others.

Setting the Context

Use these answers as needed for the question highlighted in this section.

- Proclaiming the gospel should be an encouragement for other believers so we are all constantly reminded of the grace and power of God in Jesus to save us.
- Christians proclaim the gospel in the world as a joyful obedience and privilege because of what God has done for us.
- No matter the person or the place, we should always be looking for opportunities to share the gospel of Jesus Christ.

Use the following activity to help group members see the importance of Jesus' exaltation in His crucifixion, resurrection, and ascension.

Call attention to **"Jesus' Exaltation"** (p. 83) and ask the following questions:

- What does *exaltation* mean? *(to be lifted up, elevated)*

- What exaltation of Jesus could be missing from this list? *(Jesus' crucifixion [see John 12:32-33])*

- How does Jesus embody the biblical principle that God opposes the proud but gives grace to the humble (Prov. 3:34; Jas. 4:6; 1 Pet. 5:5)? *(The Son of God humbled Himself to take on flesh and die in the place of sinners, so God raised Him up from the dead and to His throne, and every knee will bow to Him and every tongue confess that He is Lord [see Phil. 2:5-11].)*

Continuing the Discussion

Watch this session's video, and then as part of the group discussion, use these answers as needed for the questions highlighted in this section.

Matthew 28:16-20

- Those who worship Jesus will feel compelled to live on mission for Him.
- The mission seeks to make more worshipers of Jesus Christ.
- If Jesus is not God, then He is not worthy of our worship, nor is He worthy of the gospel mission.

Acts 1:4-8

- So they had power and boldness to proclaim the gospel to a hostile world.
- So they had wisdom and the words to say when addressing all sorts of people with the gospel.
- So they knew Jesus was with them as they fulfilled the Great Commission.

Acts 1:9-11

- Jesus was returning back to the Father, where He sat down at His right hand to rule over all creation.
- Jesus' ascension in the clouds fulfilled Daniel's vision of "one like a son of man" being given an eternal kingdom (Dan. 7:13-14).
- Christians on mission serve as ambassadors of the King over all the universe, proclaiming His gospel, greatness, and praise so people will join His kingdom through repentance and faith.

Share the following statement with the group. Then direct them to record in the space provided in their book at least one way they will apply the truth of Scripture as a disciple of Jesus who will obey His Great Commission in the power of the Holy Spirit.

✚ MISSIONAL Application

Because others were obedient to Christ's command and were a part in making us disciples, we go and make disciples of all nations by declaring the truth of the gospel in the power of the Holy Spirit through our words and actions that demonstrate the reality of His love.

Close your group in prayer, praying that you would be busy about the work God has given you to as a follower of Christ.

FOR GOD LOVED
THE WORLD
IN THIS WAY:

He gave his one and only Son,
so that everyone
who believes in him
will not perish
but have eternal life.

JOHN 3:16

FROM COVER
TO COVER,

the Bible is the story of God's plan to redeem sinners through Jesus—the gospel. Gospel Foundations tells that story.

———

Be sure to take advantage of the following resources if you're planning a churchwide study. Even the *Single Group Starter Pack* offers significant savings.

CHURCH LAUNCH KIT (DIGITAL)

Want to take your entire church through Gospel Foundations? You'll want a *Church Launch Kit*. It includes sermon outlines, promotional graphics, and a Wordsearch Bible digital library for all leaders valued at $330. The *Kit* comes complimentary with every *Church Starter Pack*. Also available separately.

$29.99

———

Order online, call 800.458.2772, or visit the LifeWay Christian Store serving you.

STARTER PACKS

You can save money and time by purchasing starter packs for your group or church. Every *Church Starter Pack* includes a digital *Church Launch Kit* and access to a digital version of the *Leader Kit* videos.

Single Group Starter Pack
(10 *Bible Study Books*, 1 *Leader Kit*)
$99.99

Church Starter Pack - Small
(50 *Bible Study Books*, 5 *Leader Kit* DVDs, *Church Launch Kit*)
$449.99

Church Starter Pack - Medium
(100 *Bible Study Books*, 10 *Leader Kit* DVDs, *Church Launch Kit*)
$799.99

Church Starter Pack - Large
(500 *Bible Study Books*, 50 *Leader Kit* DVDs, *Church Launch Kit*)
$3495.99

LifeWay.com/GospelFoundations

GOSPEL FOUNDATIONS

The Kingdom on Earth

VOL. 6	ACTS – REVELATION

A Year Through the Storyline of Scripture   LifeWay

Continue your study of the bigger story of Scripture.

———

In this final volume of Gospel Foundations, we continue our study in the New Testament and see that the gospel was on the move. The good news of God's rescue of sinners spread from a handful of followers to a multinational movement, one people made from every tribe, tongue, and nation. *The Kingdom on Earth* shows how the gospel story ends with Jesus' return and all things being made new, all of the consequences of sin being dealt with, and us enjoying eternal, unhindered relationship with God as He intended. (7 sessions)

Bible Study Book $9.99
Leader Kit $29.99

Group Directory

Name: _____   Name: _____

Home Phone: _____   Home Phone: _____

Mobile Phone: _____   Mobile Phone: _____

Email: _____   Email: _____

Social Media: _____   Social Media: _____

Name: _____   Name: _____

Home Phone: _____   Home Phone: _____

Mobile Phone: _____   Mobile Phone: _____

Email: _____   Email: _____

Social Media: _____   Social Media: _____

Name: _____   Name: _____

Home Phone: _____   Home Phone: _____

Mobile Phone: _____   Mobile Phone: _____

Email: _____   Email: _____

Social Media: _____   Social Media: _____

Name: _____   Name: _____

Home Phone: _____   Home Phone: _____

Mobile Phone: _____   Mobile Phone: _____

Email: _____   Email: _____

Social Media: _____   Social Media: _____

Name: _____   Name: _____

Home Phone: _____   Home Phone: _____

Mobile Phone: _____   Mobile Phone: _____

Email: _____   Email: _____

Social Media: _____   Social Media: _____

Name: _____   Name: _____

Home Phone: _____   Home Phone: _____

Mobile Phone: _____   Mobile Phone: _____

Email: _____   Email: _____

Social Media: _____   Social Media: _____